Francis Frith's

Around Preston

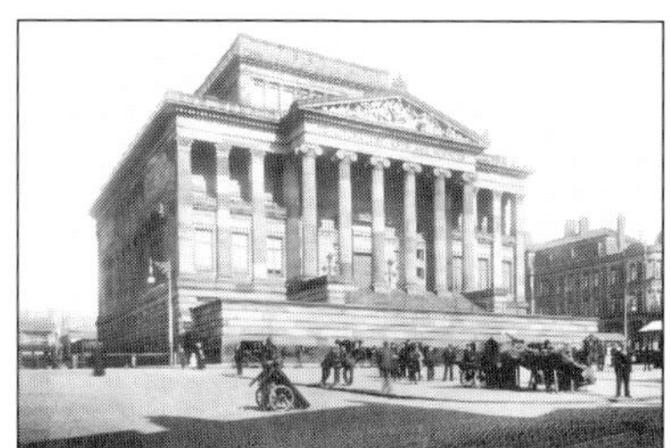

Photographic Memories

Francis Frith's

Around Preston

Cliff Hayes

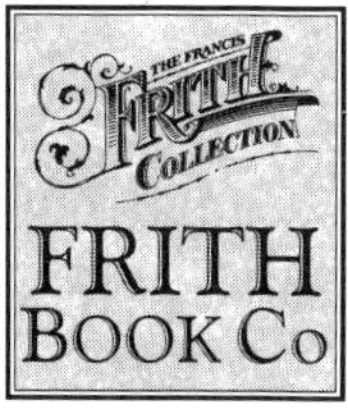

Revised paperback edition published in the United Kingdom in 2000 by
Frith Book Company Ltd

British Library Cataloguing in Publication Data

Francis Frith's
Around Preston
Cliff Hayes

ISBN 1-85937-212-0

Frith Book Company Ltd
Frith's Barn, Teffont,
Salisbury, Wiltshire SP3 5QP
Tel: +44 (0) 1722 716 376
Email: info@frithbook.co.uk
www.frithbook.co.uk

Printed and bound in Great Britain

Front Cover: **Fishergate 1903** 50068

As with any historical database the Frith archive is constantly being corrected and improved and the publishers would welcome information on omissions or inaccuracies

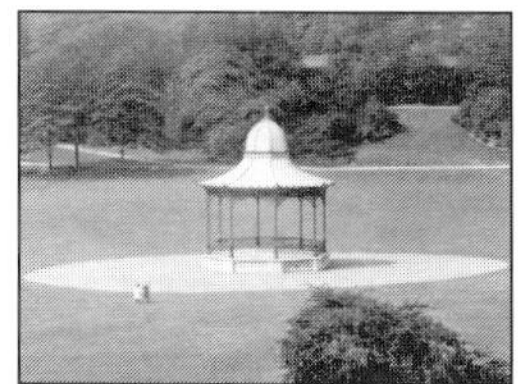

Contents

Francis Frith: *Victorian Pioneer*

FRANCIS FRITH, Victorian founder of the world-famous photographic archive, was a complex and multi-talented man. A devout Quaker and a highly successful Victorian businessman, he was both philosophic by nature and pioneering in outlook.

By 1855 Francis Frith had already established a wholesale grocery business in Liverpool, and sold it for the astonishing sum of £200,000, which is the equivalent today of over £15,000,000. Now a multi-millionaire, he was able to indulge his passion for travel. As a child he had pored over travel books written by early explorers, and his fancy and imagination had been stirred by family holidays to the sublime mountain regions of Wales and Scotland. 'What a land of spirit-stirring and enriching scenes and places!' he had written. He was to return to these scenes of grandeur in later years to 'recapture the thousands of vivid and tender memories', but with a different purpose. Now in his thirties, and captivated by the new science of photography, Frith set out on a series of pioneering journeys to the Nile regions that occupied him from 1856 until 1860.

Intrigue and Adventure

He took with him on his travels a specially-designed wicker carriage that acted as both dark-room and sleeping chamber. These far-flung journeys were packed with intrigue and adventure. In his life story, written when he was sixty-three, Frith tells of being held captive by bandits, and of fighting 'an awful midnight battle to the very point of surrender with a deadly pack of hungry, wild dogs'. Sporting flowing Arab costume, Frith arrived at Akaba by camel seventy years before Lawrence, where he encountered 'desert princes and rival sheikhs, blazing with jewel-hilted swords'.

During these extraordinary adventures he was assiduously exploring the desert regions bordering the Nile and patiently recording the antiquities and peoples with his camera. He was the first photographer to venture beyond the sixth cataract. Africa was still the mysterious 'Dark Continent', and Stanley and Livingstone's historic meeting was a decade into the future. The conditions for picture taking confound belief. He laboured for hours in his wicker dark-room in the sweltering heat of the desert, while the volatile chemicals fizzed dangerously in their trays. Often he was forced to work in remote tombs and caves where conditions were cooler. Back in London he exhibited his photographs and was 'rapturously cheered' by members of the Royal Society. His reputation as a photographer was made overnight. An eminent modern historian has likened their impact on the population of the time to that on our own generation of the first photographs taken on the surface of the moon.

Venture of a Life-Time

Characteristically, Frith quickly spotted the opportunity to create a new business as a specialist publisher of photographs. He lived in an era of immense and sometimes violent change. For the poor in the early part of Victoria's reign work was a drudge and the hours long, and people had precious little free time to enjoy themselves. Most had no transport other than a cart or gig at their disposal, and had not travelled far beyond the boundaries of their own town or village. However, by the 1870s, the railways had threaded their way across the country, and Bank Holidays and half-day Saturdays had been made obligatory by Act of Parliament. All of a sudden the ordinary working man and his family were able to enjoy days out and see a little more of the world.

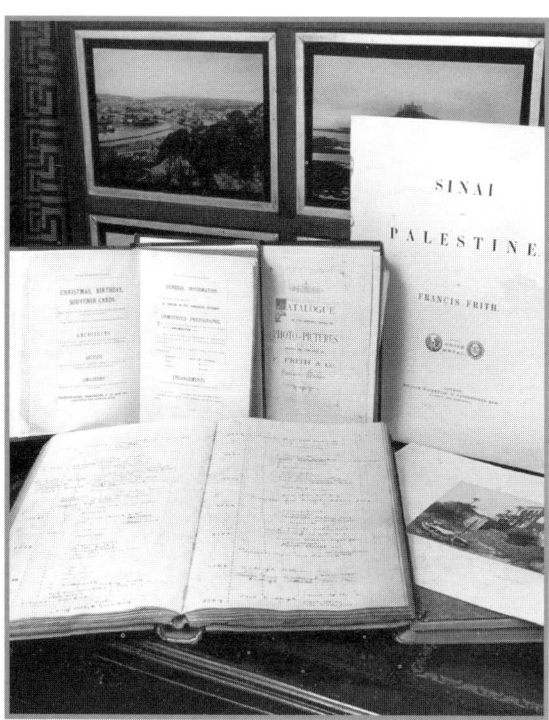

With characteristic business acumen, Francis Frith foresaw that these new tourists would enjoy having souvenirs to commemorate their days out. In 1860 he married Mary Ann Rosling and set out with the intention of photographing every city, town and village in Britain. For the next thirty years he travelled the country by train and by pony and trap, producing fine photographs of seaside resorts and beauty spots that were keenly bought by millions of Victorians. These prints were painstakingly pasted into family albums and pored over during the dark nights of winter, rekindling precious memories of summer excursions.

The Rise of Frith & Co

Frith's studio was soon supplying retail shops all over the country. To meet the demand he gathered about him a small team of photographers, and published the work of independent artist-photographers of the calibre of Roger Fenton and Francis Bedford. In order to gain some understanding of the scale of Frith's business one only has to look at the catalogue issued by Frith & Co in 1886: it runs to some 670 pages, listing not only many thousands of views of the British Isles but also many photographs of most European countries, and China, Japan, the USA and

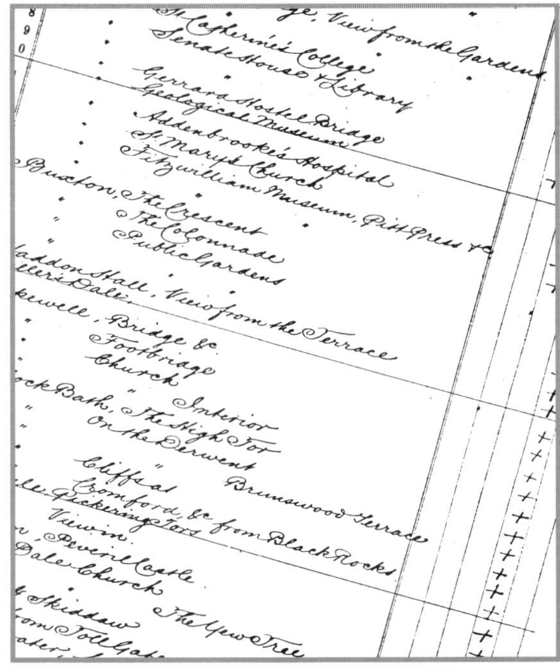
St Catherine's College ge, View from the Gardens
Senate House & Library
Gerrard Hostel Bridge
Geological Museum
Addenbrooke's Hospital
St Mary's Church
Fitzwilliam Museum, Pitt Press &c
uxton, The Crescent
The Colonnade
Public Gardens
addon Hall, View from the Terrace
kewell, Bridge &c
Footbridge
Church
ck Bath, The High Tor
Interior
On the Derwent
Cliffs at
Brunswood Terrace
Cromford, &c from Black Rocks
Pickering Tors
View in
Peveril Castle
Dale Church
Skiddaw
The Yew Tree
om Toll Gate

Canada – note the sample page shown above from the hand-written *Frith & Co* ledgers detailing pictures taken. By 1890 Frith had created the greatest specialist photographic publishing company in the world, with over 2,000 outlets – more than the combined number that Boots and WH Smith have today! The picture on the right shows the *Frith & Co* display board at Ingleton in the Yorkshire Dales. Beautifully constructed with mahogany frame and gilt inserts, it could display up to a dozen local scenes.

Postcard Bonanza

The ever-popular holiday postcard we know today took many years to develop. In 1870 the Post Office issued the first plain cards, with a pre-printed stamp on one face. In 1894 they allowed other publishers' cards to be sent through the mail with an attached adhesive halfpenny stamp. Demand grew rapidly, and in 1895 a new size of postcard was permitted called the court card, but there was little room for illustration. In 1899, a year after Frith's death, a new card measuring 5.5 x 3.5 inches became the standard format, but it was not until 1902 that the divided back came into being, with address and message on one face and a full-size illustration on the other. *Frith & Co* were in the vanguard of postcard development, and Frith's sons Eustace and Cyril continued their father's monumental task, expanding the number of views offered to the public and recording more and more places in Britain, as the coasts and countryside were opened up to mass travel.

Francis Frith died in 1898 at his villa in Cannes, his great project still growing. The archive he created continued in business for another seventy years. By 1970 it contained over a third of a million pictures of 7,000 cities, towns and villages. The massive photographic record Frith has left to us stands as a living monument to a special and very remarkable man.

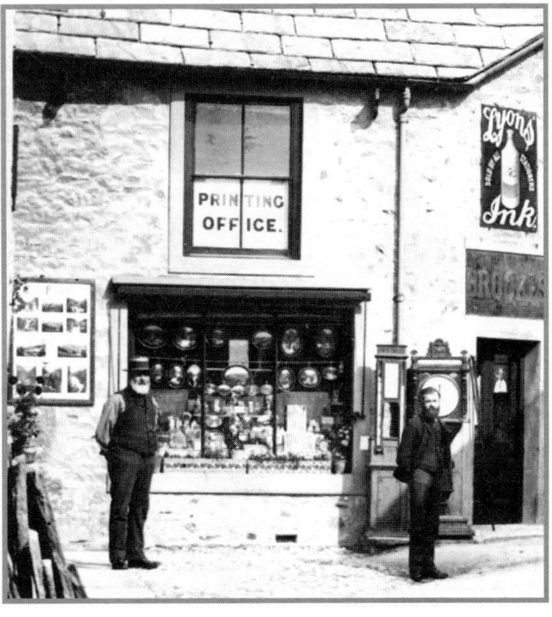

Frith's Archive: *A Unique Legacy*

Francis Frith's legacy to us today is of immense significance and value, for the magnificent archive of evocative photographs he created provides a unique record of change in 7,000 cities, towns and villages throughout Britain over a century and more. Frith and his fellow studio photographers revisited locations many times down the years to update their views, compiling for us an enthralling and colourful pageant of British life and character.

We tend to think of Frith's sepia views of Britain as nostalgic, for most of us use them to conjure up memories of places in our own lives with which we have family associations. It often makes us forget that to Francis Frith they were records of daily life as it was actually being lived in the cities, towns and villages of his day. The Victorian age was one of great and often bewildering change for ordinary people, and though the pictures evoke an impression of slower times, life was as busy and hectic as it is today.

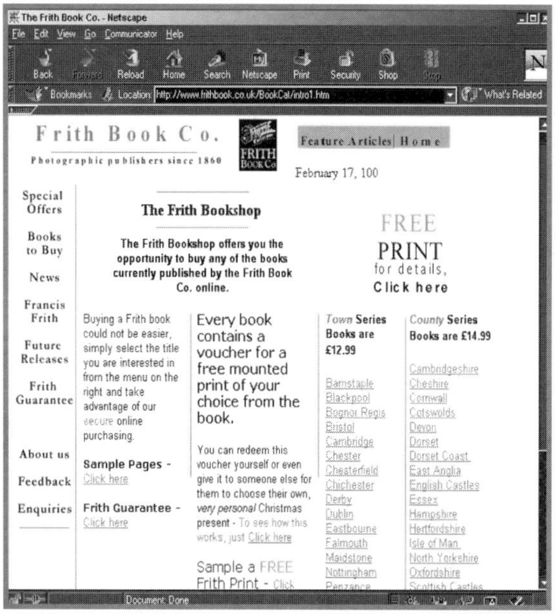

We are fortunate that Frith was a photographer of the people, dedicated to recording the minutiae of everyday life. For it is this sheer wealth of visual data, the painstaking chronicle of changes in dress, transport, street layouts, buildings, housing, engineering and landscape that captivates us so much today. His remarkable images offer us a powerful link with the past and with the lives of our ancestors.

See Frith at www. frithbook.co.uk

Today's Technology

Computers have now made it possible for Frith's many thousands of images to be accessed almost instantly. In the Frith archive today, each photograph is carefully 'digitised' then stored on a CD Rom. Frith archivists can locate a single photograph amongst thousands within seconds. Views can be catalogued and sorted under a variety of categories of place and content to the immediate benefit of researchers.

Inexpensive reference prints can be created for them at the touch of a mouse button, and a wide range of books and other printed materials assembled and published for a wider, more general readership - in the next twelve months over a hundred Frith local history titles will be published! The day-to-day workings of the archive are very different from how they were in Francis Frith's time: imagine the herculean task of sorting through eleven tons of glass negatives as Frith had to do to locate a particular sequence of pictures! Yet the archive still prides itself on maintaining the same high standards of excellence laid down by Francis Frith, including the painstaking cataloguing and indexing of every view.

It is curious to reflect on how the internet now allows researchers in America and elsewhere greater instant access to the archive than Frith himself ever enjoyed. Many thousands of individual views can be called up on screen within seconds on one of the Frith internet sites, enabling people living continents away to revisit the streets of their ancestral home town, or view places in Britain where they have enjoyed holidays. Many overseas researchers welcome the chance to view special theme selections, such as transport, sports, costume and ancient monuments.

We are certain that Francis Frith would have heartily approved of these modern developments in imaging techniques, for he himself was always working at the very limits of Victorian photographic technology.

The Value of the Archive Today

Because of the benefits brought by the computer, Frith's images are increasingly studied by social historians, by researchers into genealogy and ancestory, by architects, town planners, and by teachers and schoolchildren involved in local history projects.

In addition, the archive offers every one of us an opportunity to examine the places where we and our families have lived and worked down the years. Highly successful in Frith's own era, the archive is now, a century and more on, entering a new phase of popularity.

The Past in Tune with the Future

Historians consider the Francis Frith Collection to be of prime national importance. It is the only archive of its kind remaining in private ownership and has been valued at a million pounds. However, this figure is now rapidly increasing as digital technology enables more and more people around the world to enjoy its benefits.

Francis Frith's archive is now housed in an historic timber barn in the beautiful village of Teffont in Wiltshire. Its founder would not recognize the archive office as it is today. In place of the many thousands of dusty boxes containing glass plate negatives and an all-pervading odour of photographic chemicals, there are now ranks of computer screens. He would be amazed to watch his images travelling round the world at unimaginable speeds through network and internet lines.

The archive's future is both bright and exciting. Francis Frith, with his unshakeable belief in making photographs available to the greatest number of people, would undoubtedly approve of what is being done today with his lifetime's work. His photographs, depicting our shared past, are now bringing pleasure and enlightenment to millions around the world a century and more after his death.

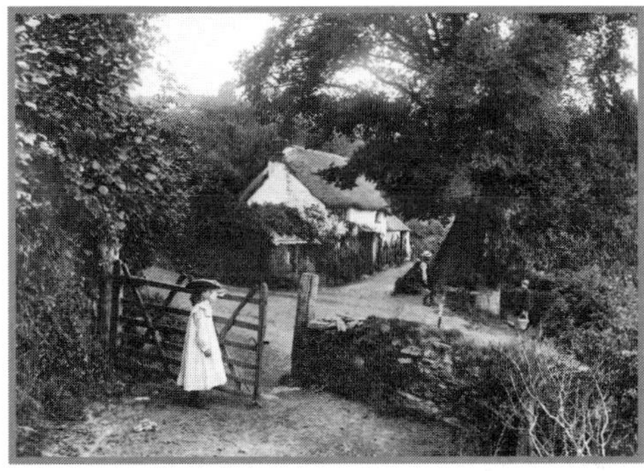

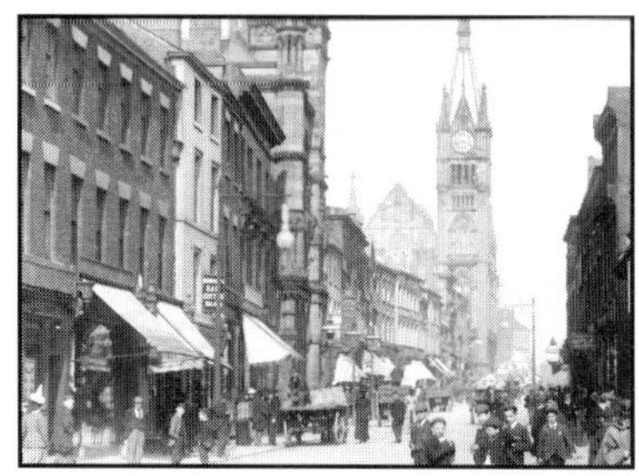

Proud Preston

THE ROMANS DO not appear to have occupied the area that is Preston. Roman coins and bits of pottery have been found around Preston, but it was out at Ribchester and Walton that they had their forts. One theory is that the River Ribble ran much deeper and faster in Roman times, and fording the river at this point would have been too dangerous.

Tradition states that Athelstan, King of the Mercians and West Saxons, the grandson of Alfred the Great, passed through Preston capturing all before him on his way to beat the Danish invaders in Northumberland. The monks from Ripon, who accompanied him, prayed for his soul, and for strength to conquer the enemy. For this they were granted the town of Preston. Later, the town was transferred to the ownership of the Archbishop of York, which seems hard to believe now. During the Danish invasions of York, Yorkshire lost its grip on the town, and Harold II's brother Tosti was given Preston as an income.

After the Norman conquest, the town, along with much of the area of the Ribble Valley, passed to Roger de Pictou, one of the great Norman barons and friend of William the Conqueror. In 1339, after Lancaster backed the wrong side in one of the power struggles of the time, Edward III took Preston under royal protection, and it was then that a municipal form of rule was established.

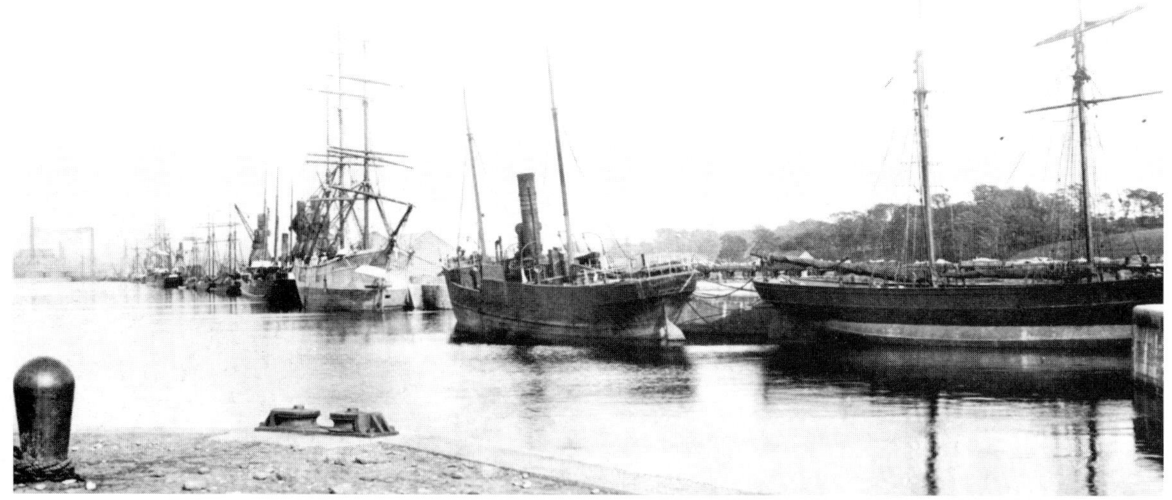

Preston was the principal town in the Hundred of Amounderness. Because Preston is so ideally situated, it has always figured large in the plans of people travelling north or south to and from Scotland. It is half-way up Lancashire, so this position made it an ideal compromise between the old seat of government, Lancaster, and the emerging power-houses of industry and commerce in the north-west, most notably in Warrington, Manchester and the surrounding towns. Preston is roughly half-way between London and Glasgow, so early travellers had to make a stop here. It was always a thorn in Preston's side that some of its early visitors came expecting the refinements of the larger cities, and did not leave with the right impression of the town.

The name Preston means 'the fortified enclosed place of priests'. Many say St Wilfrid was the first to mention the town in writing in 1086 as Prestone. In 1094 it was spelt as it is now, but by 1179-80 it was Presteton or de Prestona. From then on it has stayed more or less as it is today, but we do find Prestun and Prestona in old documents.

Preston was a supporter of the Jacobite cause and the Roman Catholic movement, which in turn was supported by the older Lancashire families. When James VI of Scotland became James I of England, he stayed a few days in Preston on his journey south in 1617. He is said to have had dinner at Hoghton Tower; he liked the loin of beef that he was served so much that he knighted it 'Sir Loin'. In 1323 Robert Bruce descended on Preston and burnt it. The Battle of Preston took place on 17 August 1648, when Oliver Cromwell himself led the Parliamentary army to drive off the Scots/Royalist Army under the Duke of Hamilton. They battled it out on Ribbleton Moor; even though a large part of the Royalists fled south, Cromwell caught them at Wigan and inflicted severe casualties again.

Twice in history a King James III has been proclaimed in the Square at Preston, yet a James III never made it to the throne. In 1715 on November 10, the Earl of Derwentwater and his army were in the Square, paying tribute to James III. Two days later, the Georgian royal forces arrived, and Preston was under siege. More Royalists arrived the next day, and the overwhelming number of troops meant that the siege was soon over. Fifty-eight rebels were hanged at Gallows Hill in the winter that followed. The spot later became the Roman Catholic Church of the English Martyrs, a strange twist of fate - it was the Catholic faith that the rebels were trying to restore. Just thirty years later, almost to the day, Bonnie Prince Charlie was in the Square; he declared his father, The Old Pretender, as James III. He left for Manchester with Lord Townley and

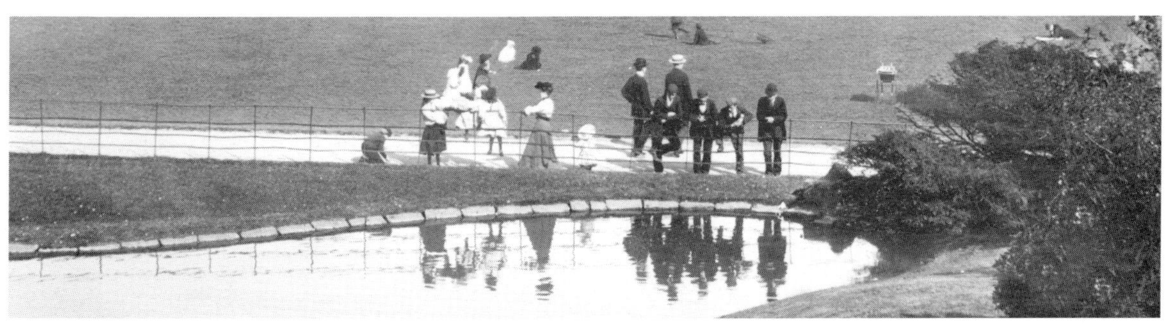

a few volunteers who had joined his 'Scotch Army'. He was soon back and in retreat, and that was the end of the Jacobite Rebellion. Since then, Preston seems to have stayed out of trouble.

Many people feel that Preston should be a city, and it has tried for many years now to attain that status. It has had Parliamentary representation since 1295 or even earlier. The Temperance Movement was put on to a formal footing in Preston, and the word T-Total was first coined here. The first Temperance Hotel opened here, and the first Temperance newspaper was published.

Over the years Preston has always been associated with Guilds, and Guild Processions are held every 20 years: hence the saying 'Every Preston Guild'. The Saxons introduced Guilds into this country. They were formal groups of like-minded individuals linked in trade. The word guild comes from an Anglo-Saxon word, 'gildan', meaning 'to pay'. In fact, the Guild system was not unlike present day insurance schemes. When you were young and strong, you paid in, when you were working and prosperous, you paid in, and in times of adversity, or when old age made it hard for you, your Guild would look after you and yours. Many a merchant slept easier in his bed knowing that if he did not wake up next morning the Guild would see that he received a decent funeral and that prayers would be said for his soul, and all the rights of burial would be given. The scope of the Guilds changed over the years: they also protected their individual crafts to make sure that standards were maintained and that working practices were fair and just. The first record of a Guild dates from 1328, although permission to form a Guild Merchant is mentioned in Henry II's Charter of c1180.

Between 1328 and 1542 the Guilds paraded the town only infrequently. After that they took place every twenty years for four centuries, with only the 1942 parade being cancelled owing to the War. It was held instead in 1952, ten years later; the next parade was held another twenty years after that in 1972, and the next in 1992, so that the next one is due in the year 2012. But why not restore the dates to their ancient place, 02, 22, 42, and so on? This would give Preston a Millennium Celebration in 2002.

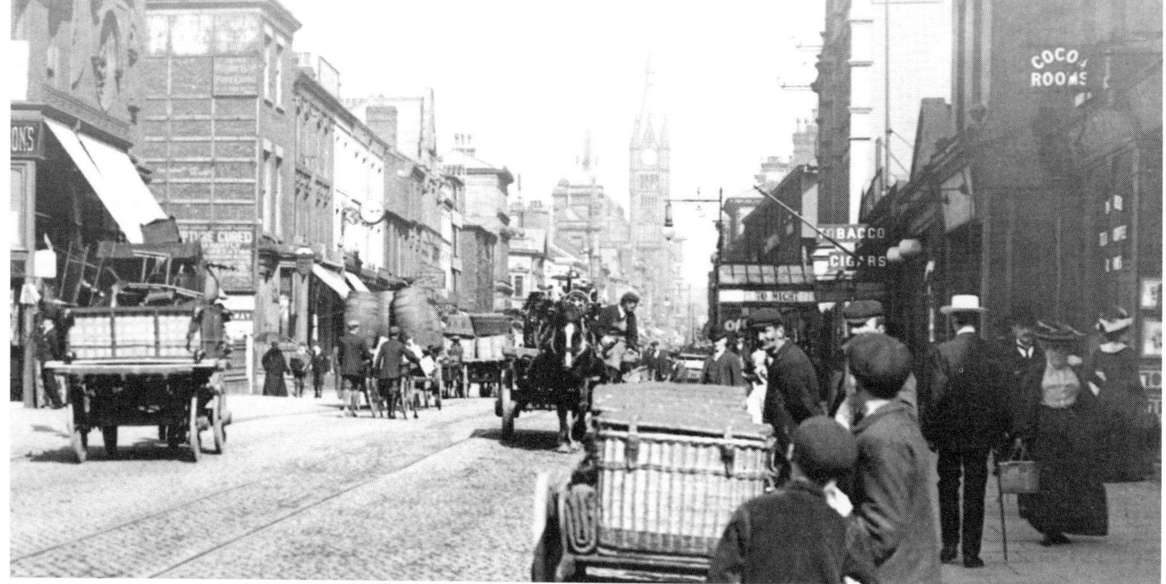

The Royal Charters

Some towns proudly boast of the date they were granted a charter: Preston was granted a charter in about 1179/80 by Henry II. That Charter has since been lost or misplaced, but it is not the only charter Preston was granted. In fact, Preston has been granted 14 charters:

1179 (Missing) King Henry II grants rights to 'Guild Merchants with all the liberties and free customs attached'.

1199 King John confirms the Charter of Henry II.

1227 (Missing) Henry III confirms previous charters.

1252 (Missing) Henry grants land at Fulwood.

1328 (Missing) Edward III confirms all previous charters.

1379 King Richard II confirms previous charters.

1401 King Henry IV confirms previous charters.

1448 King Henry V grants Charter.

1525 King Henry VI grants Charter.

1558 Philip and Mary (some historians say Queen Mary in 1557) confirm previous charters.

1566 Queen Elizabeth grants the 'Great Charter'. This incorporates the names 'Mayor', 'Bailiffs' and 'Burgesses' of the Borough of Preston and grants certain privileges.

1662 Charles II Confirmatory Charter. All offices must swear the Oath of Obedience and Oath of Supremacy.

1685 Charles II confirms the previous charter after the troubles.

1828 George IV orders there be three Coroners, the Mayor, the retiring Mayor and the senior Alderman, and the same three plus the Recorder and all Aldermen shall be ex-officio Justice of the Peace.

Thus there were many charters granted to Preston, and they were well paid for. The Guild Merchants paid the Guild, and the Guild paid the King (or Queen) for the renewal of them.

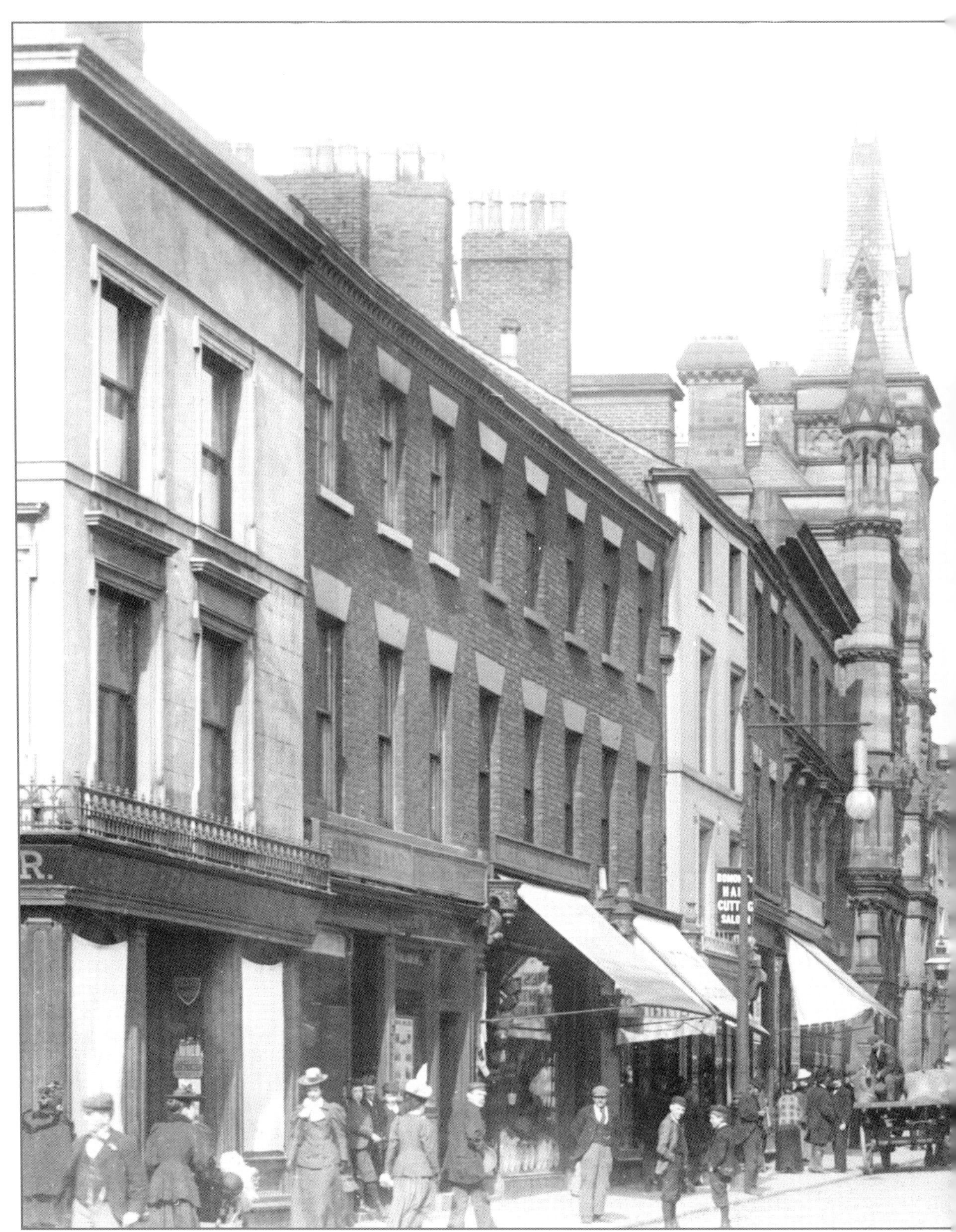

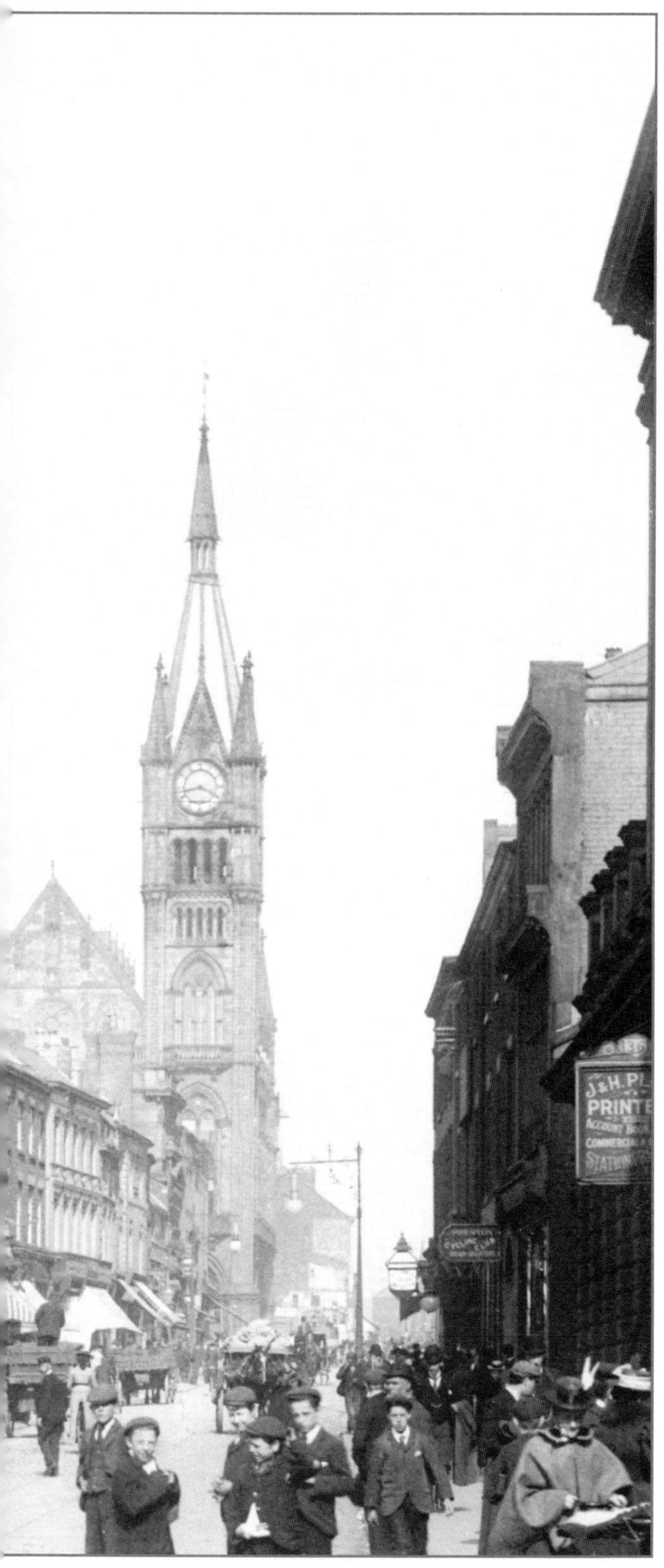

The Town

Fishergate 1898 40994
We are looking up a busy and full Fishergate from the railway station. It is hard to imagine that less than a century before this picture was taken, there was not one business or shop premises to be seen; the whole area of Fishergate consisted of private housing. The names of Preston's Gates (Friargate, Churchgate) comes from 'gata', an Anglo-Saxon word for 'the road to'; thus, Fishergate is 'the way to the fishermen or fishing place', and Friargate is 'the way to the Friary'. The hair cutting saloon and public house on the right of the street mingle with the printer's, draper's and florist's shops.

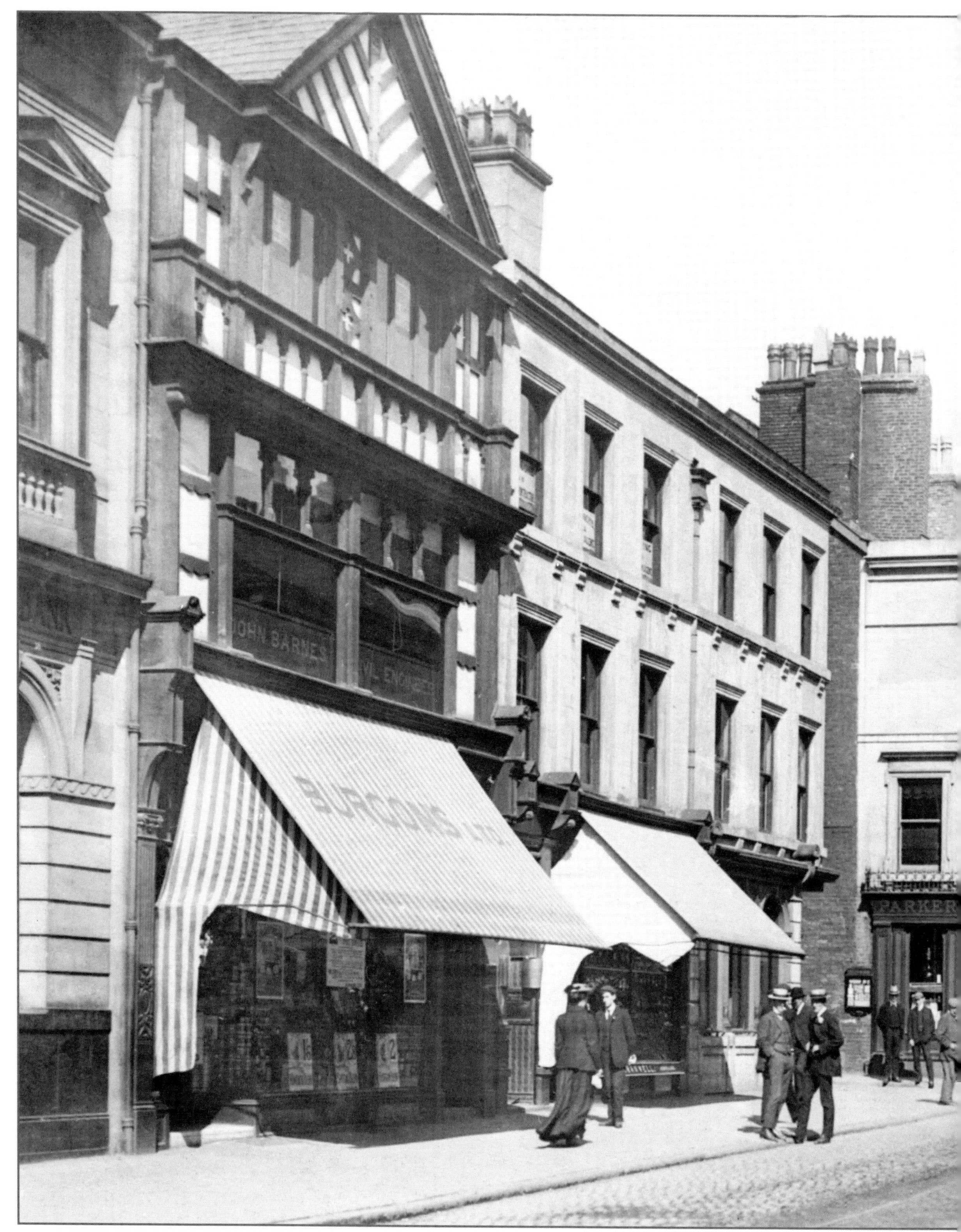
JOHN BARNES
BURGONS LTD
PARKER

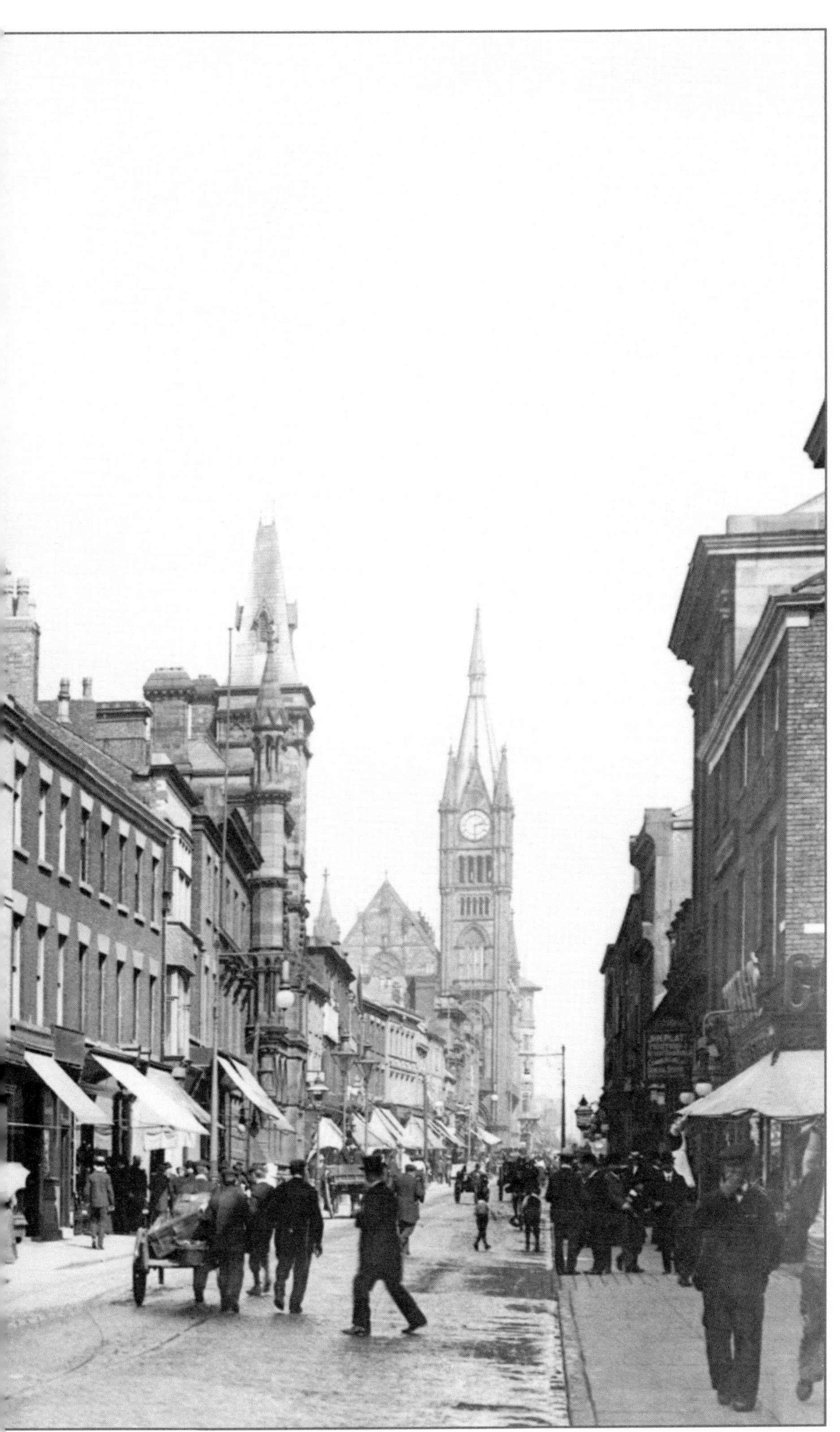

Fishergate 1903

50068

The gentlemen in their boaters and bowlers and workmen in their flat caps dominate the scene. The town hall tower with its clock rises at the far end of the street. The other tower is that of the Fishergate Baptist Church, and it can just be seen here in the middle of the picture behind the shops. Nearer the camera on the left you can see Burgons Ltd, the grocers, with its striped awning.

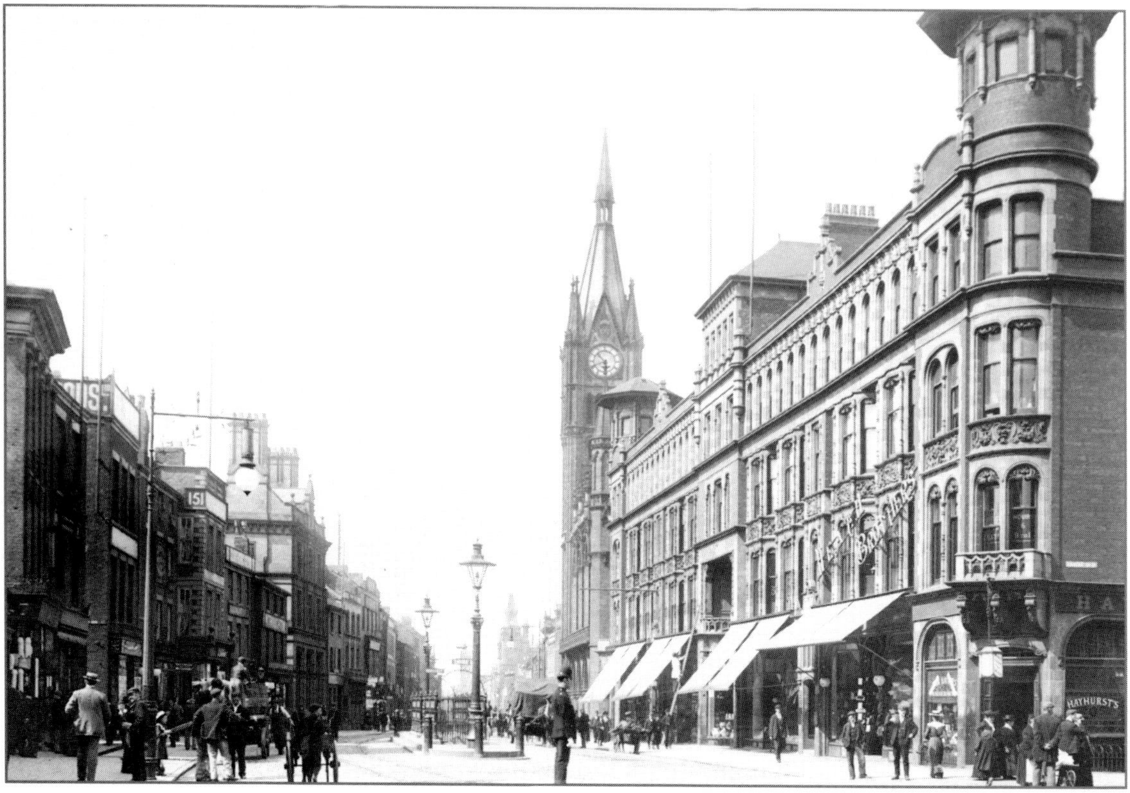

Church Street 1903 50069

We are standing in Church Street at the spot where it meets Fishergate, with Tithebarn Street on the right. On the right we see Miller's Arcade. This fine building was built by the same man who gave the land for Miller's Park. The town hall spire with its large clock face is in the centre, and we can see the old Victorian gents' toilets in the middle of the street with two ornate gas lamps at either end. There was a balcony built into the front of Miller's Arcade so that crowds below could be addressed if the need arose. Hayhurst's Wine Merchants is on the corner.

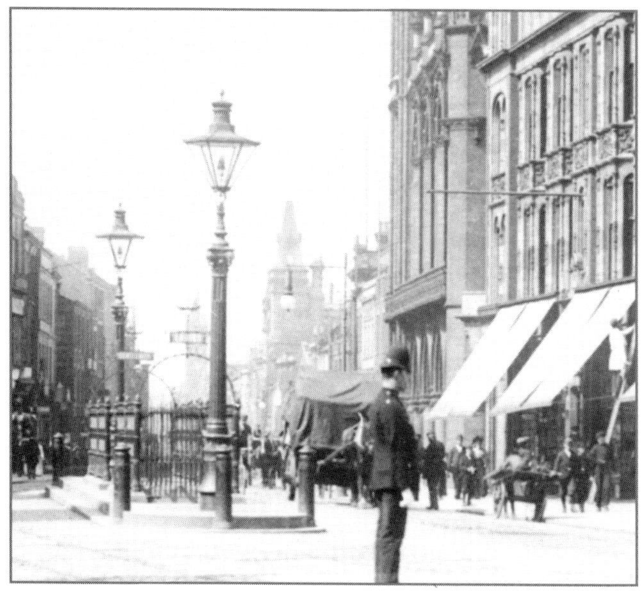

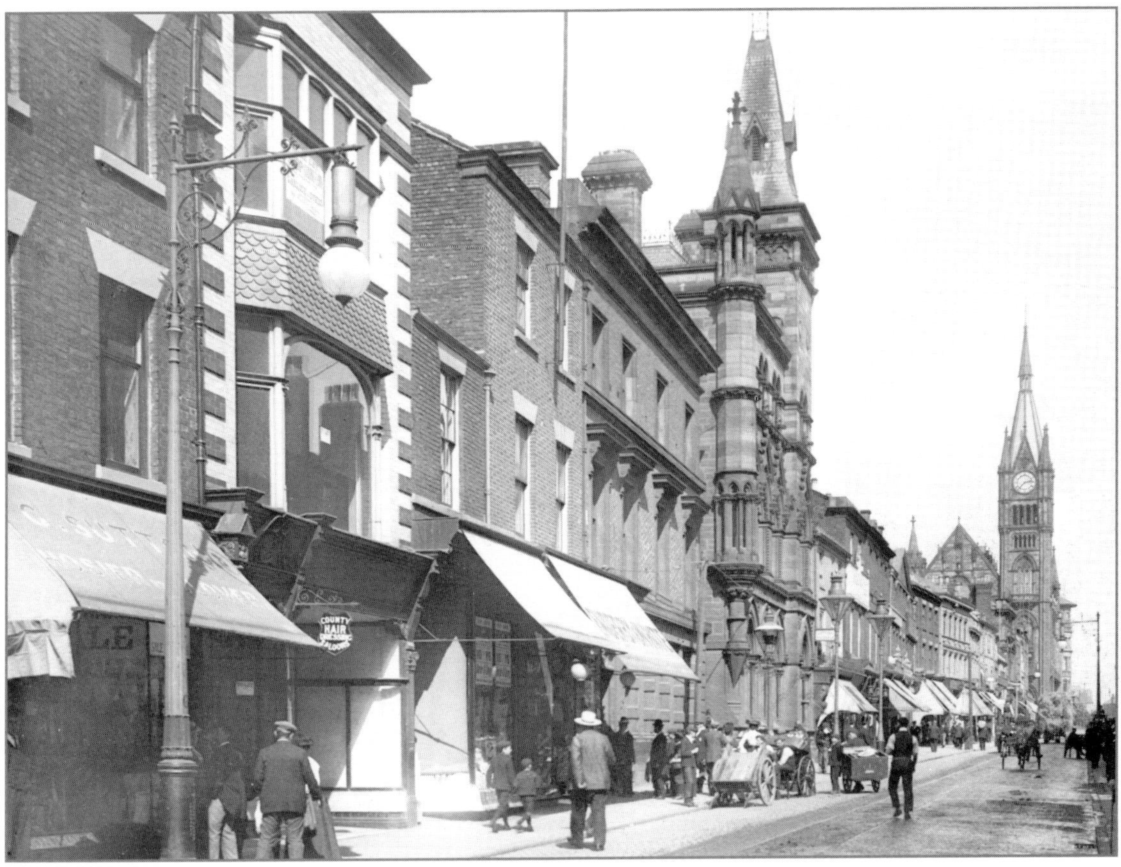

Fishergate 1903 50066

This is a close-up of the many and varied shops that graced Fishergate just a year after the first Preston Guild of the 20th century. G Sutton, Hosier & Glover is first on the left, then the County Hair Dressing Saloons. Lingard Hatter & Outfitter was just by the Baptist Church; their two best-selling lines when our photograph was taken were boaters from 1s 6d to 6s 6d and the 'Stanley' top hat, 10s 6d to a guinea. One thing not mentioned is the tunnel that ran under Fishergate at this point. It was built for the tramway which connected the Lancaster Canal with Walton. It was used as a tramway for about thirty years; it remained for over a century, and was only filled in when the St George's Centre was built.

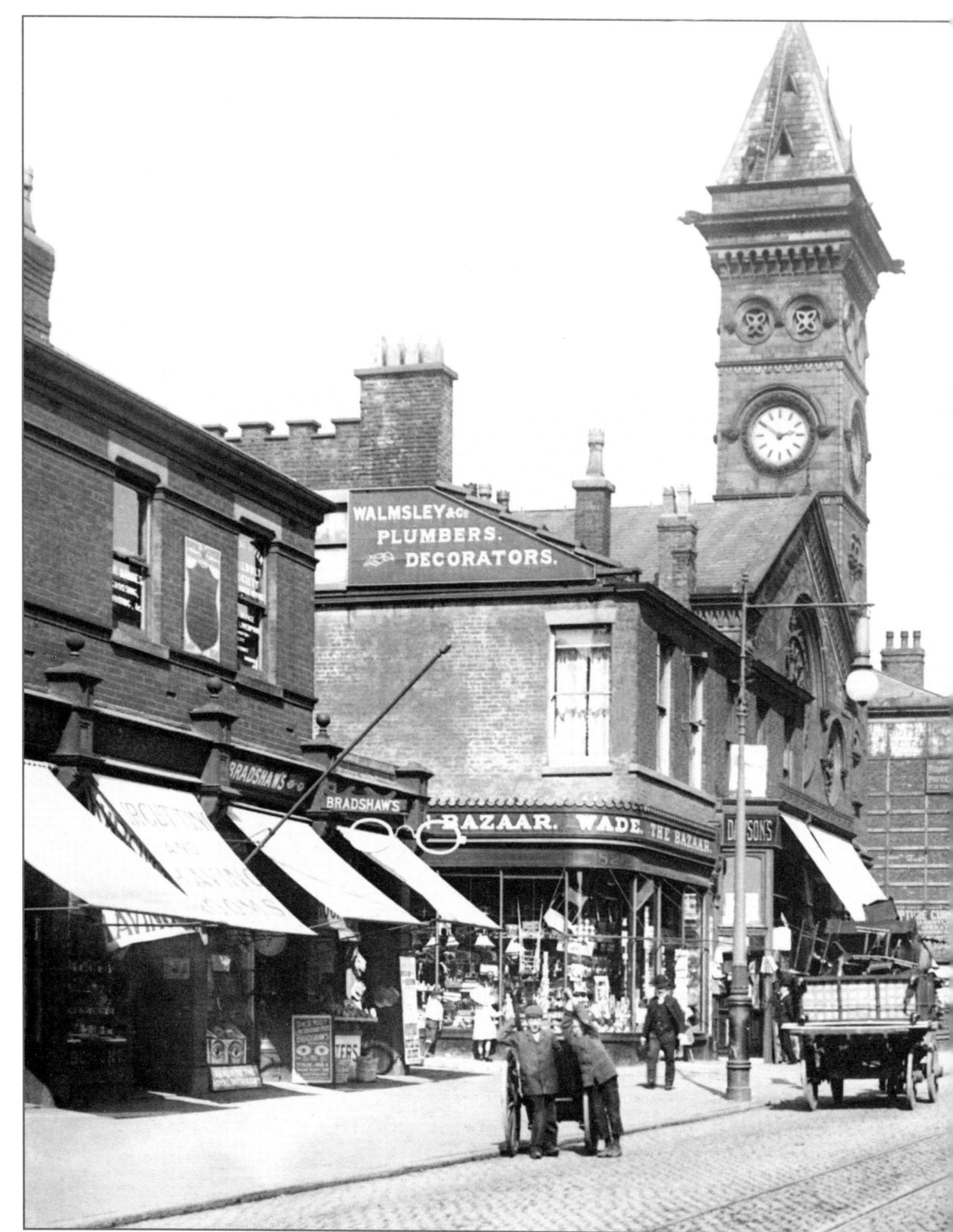
WALMSLEY & Co
PLUMBERS.
DECORATORS.
BRADSHAWS
BRADSHAW'S
BAZAAR. WADE. THE BAZAAR.

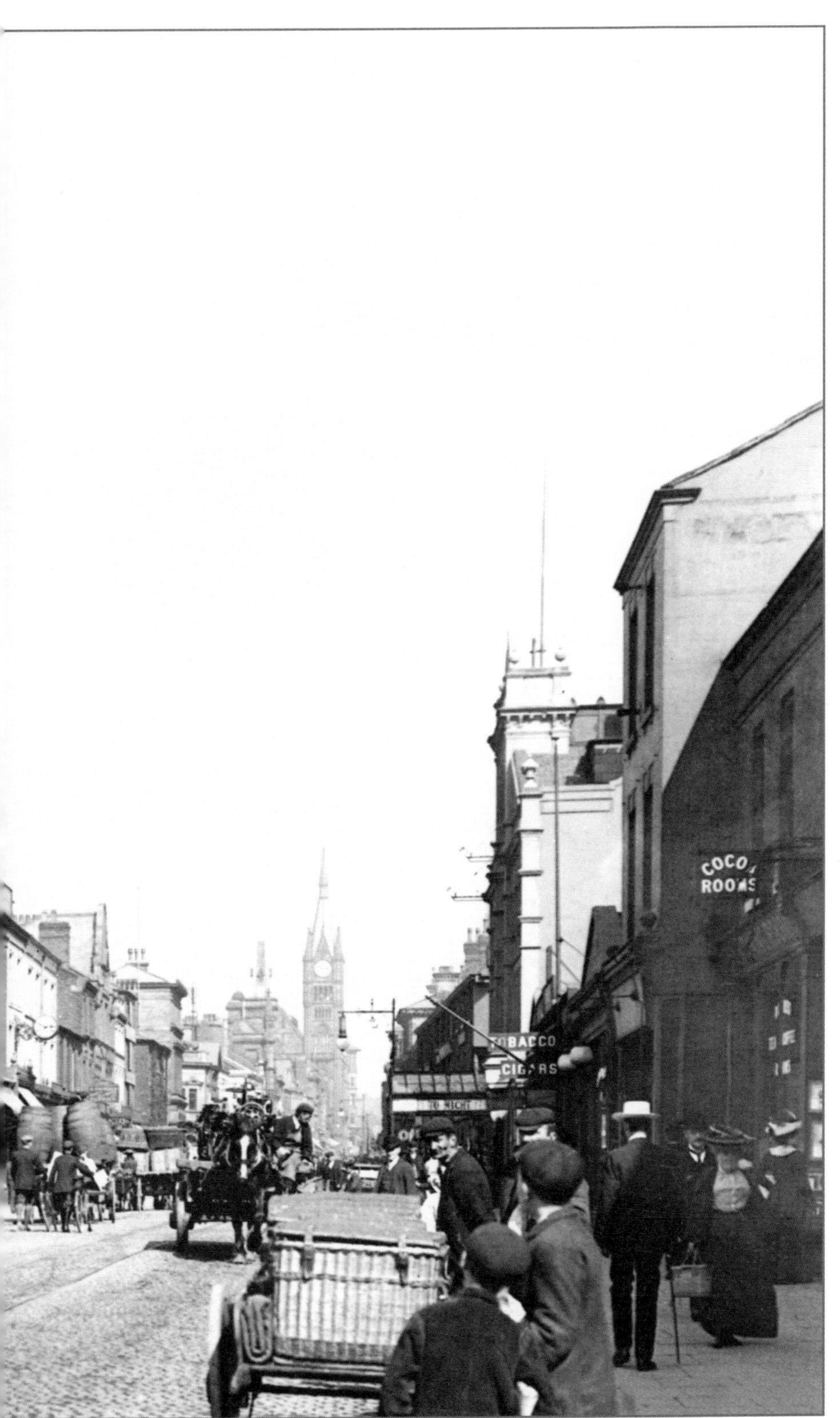

Fishergate 1903
50065
In this picture we can see the Baptist Church Tower well; it had a clock with at least three faces. This was quite unusual for a Baptist Church. Bradshaw's the Opticians and Walmsley & Co, Plumbers & Decorators, stand out on the left, and the Cocoa Rooms are on the right.

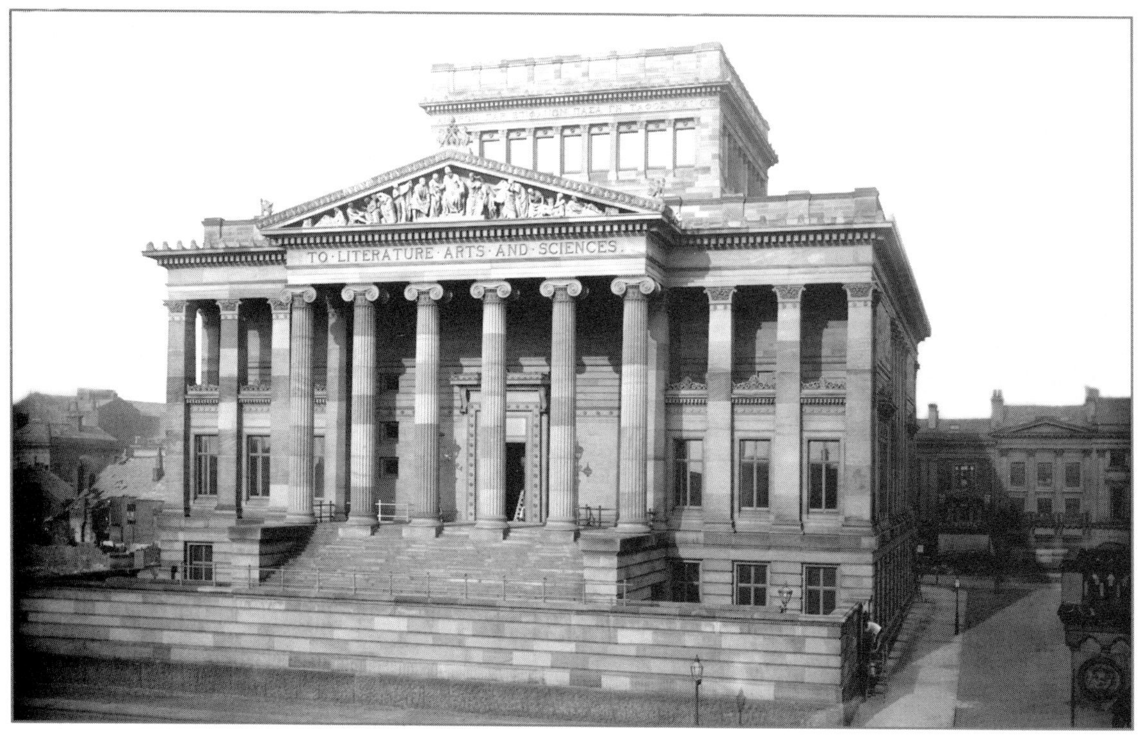

The Harris Public Library and Museum 1893 33087
Preston owes a lot to E R Harris, a minister's son who died leaving £300,000 to his native town in 1877. That is the equivalent of about £100,000,000 today. Edmund Robert Harris was the elder son of the Rev R. Harris, Vicar of St George's Church, Preston, for over sixty-four years. His will insisted that the money be used 'to perpetuate the remembrance of his father and his family'; the town not only got a library, but an orphanage, the Harris Institute, and much more. The site for this Library was land given by the Corporation; the foundation stone was laid during Guild Week in 1882 by Lord Lathom.

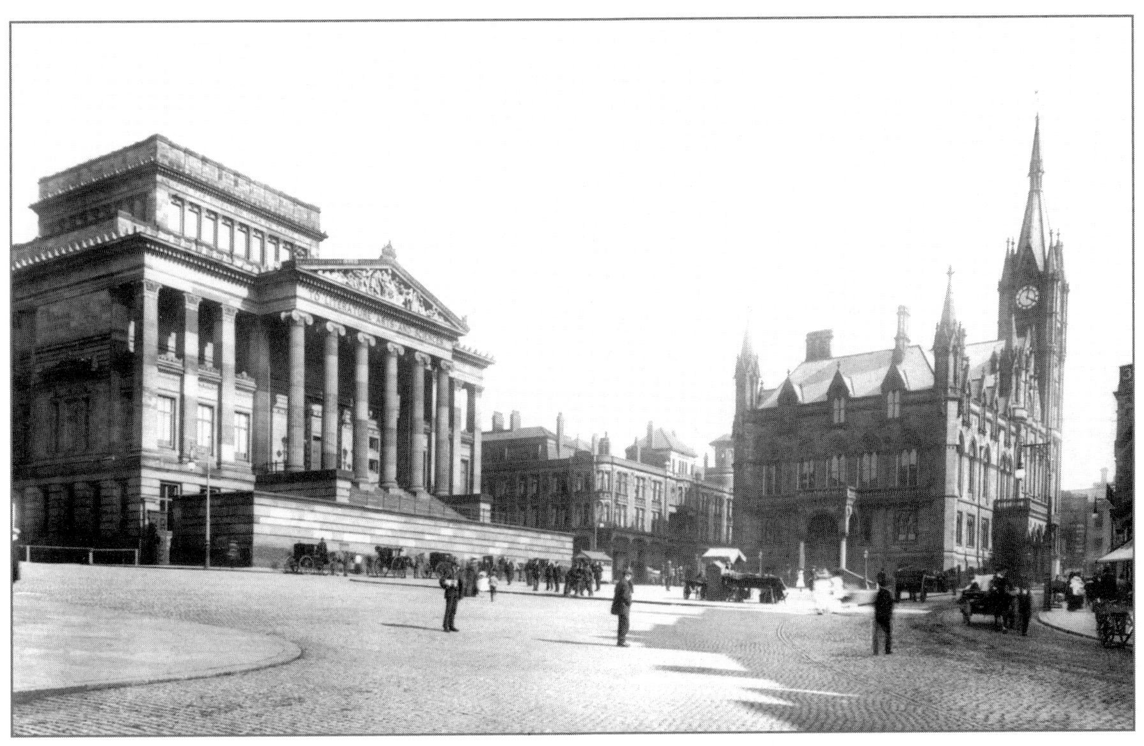

The Art Gallery and the Town Hall 1903 50084

'There is not another square in Lancashire that has such grand and gothic buildings, all vying for attention'. These words are from a century ago, and our Frith picture gives a hint as to why they were written. The town hall with its high Gothic tower is on the right, and the Harris Public Library is on the left. The Market Square has been the centre of Preston's life for many centuries; it was clever and thoughtful planning that led to the laying-out of such a large open area in the middle of town. At one time the grain market, cattle market, and linen market have all been held here, but today only the famous Preston Pot Market survives.

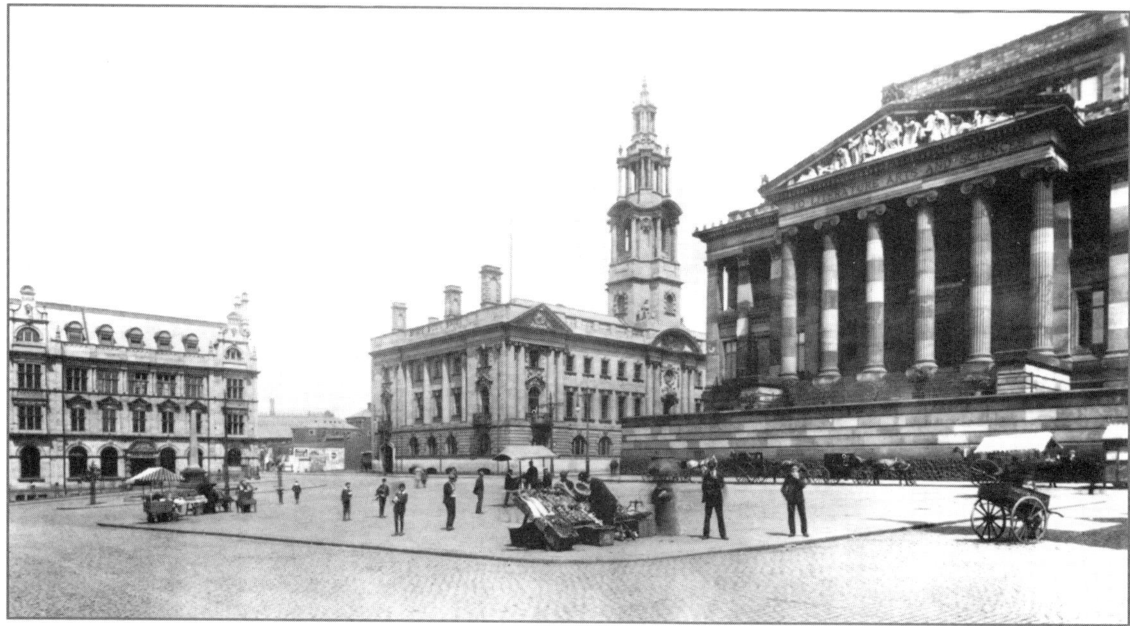

Market Square 1906 56123
The Post Office is to the left, the Harris Public Library on the right, and the County Sessions Hall in the middle. There are a few market traders plying their trade, but there are no crowds of customers - it could be early morning before business has got going. After it opened in 1893, the Harris building was just a public library, with a small section of it used as a museum. Two years later the Art Gallery opened, and the whole building came into use.

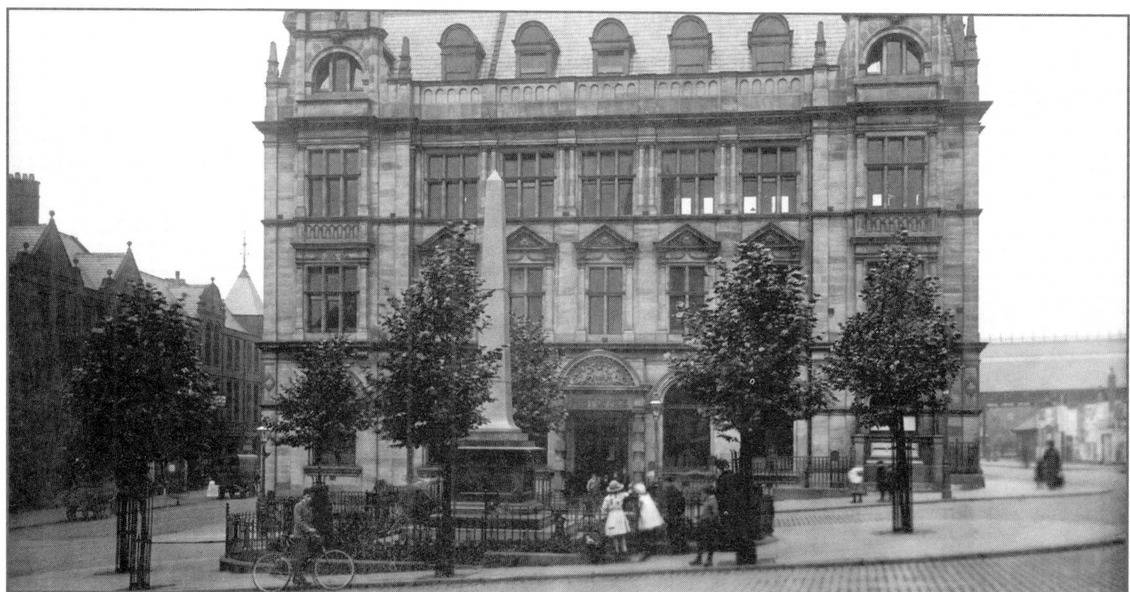

The Post Office 1913 65592
Here we have Preston's new Post Office, which opened at the turn of the last century. We can see quite clearly the Boer War Memorial at the front of the Post Office. A few years later it was moved to Avenham Park to make way for the Great War Memorial erected to honour those who lost their lives in the First World War which began just twelve months after this photograph was taken. At the time of our photograph, the Post Office opened from 7.30am to 7.30pm six days a week.

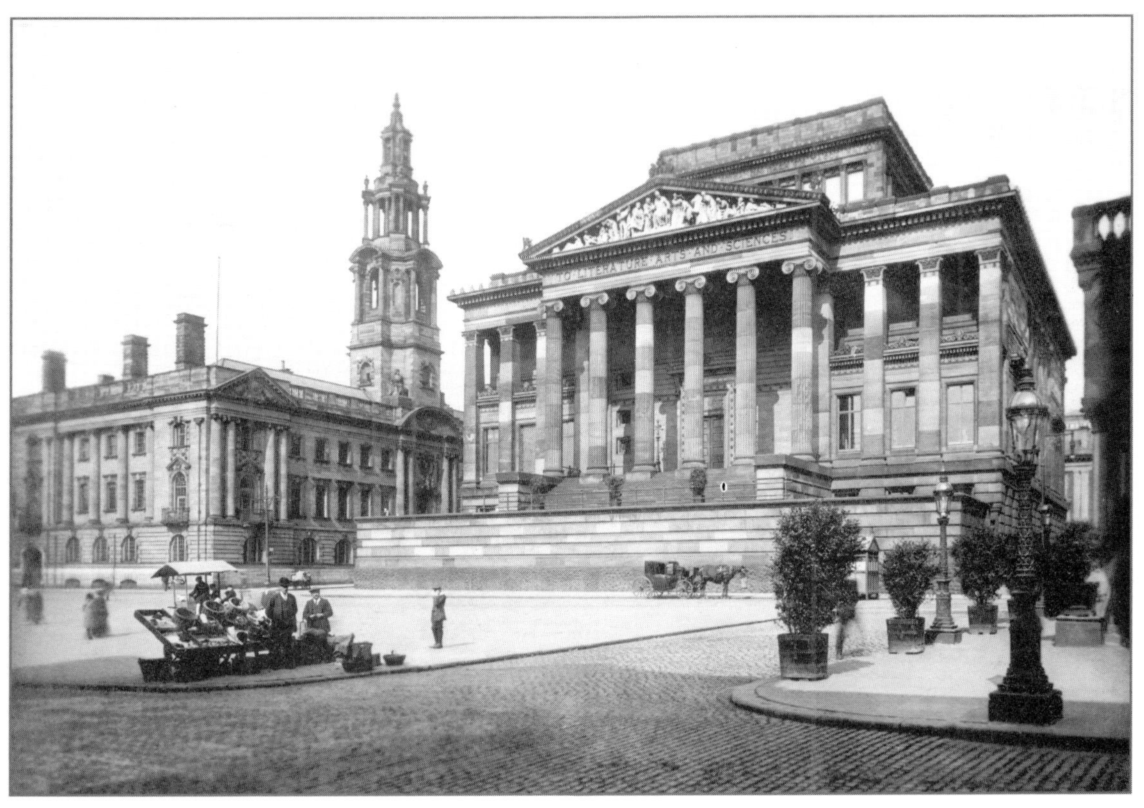

The Sessions House and the Harris Library and Art Gallery 1913 65586

The Session House is on the left, and the Harris takes up most of the picture. This is another quiet picture of the Market Square, with only one trader in sight. We also have a great view of the magnificent County Sessions House on the left, built in 1900 in English Renaissance style, and adorned with a gracefully ornate tower. These imposing buildings are a testimony to Preston's commercial wealth, and its importance in the north-west of England.

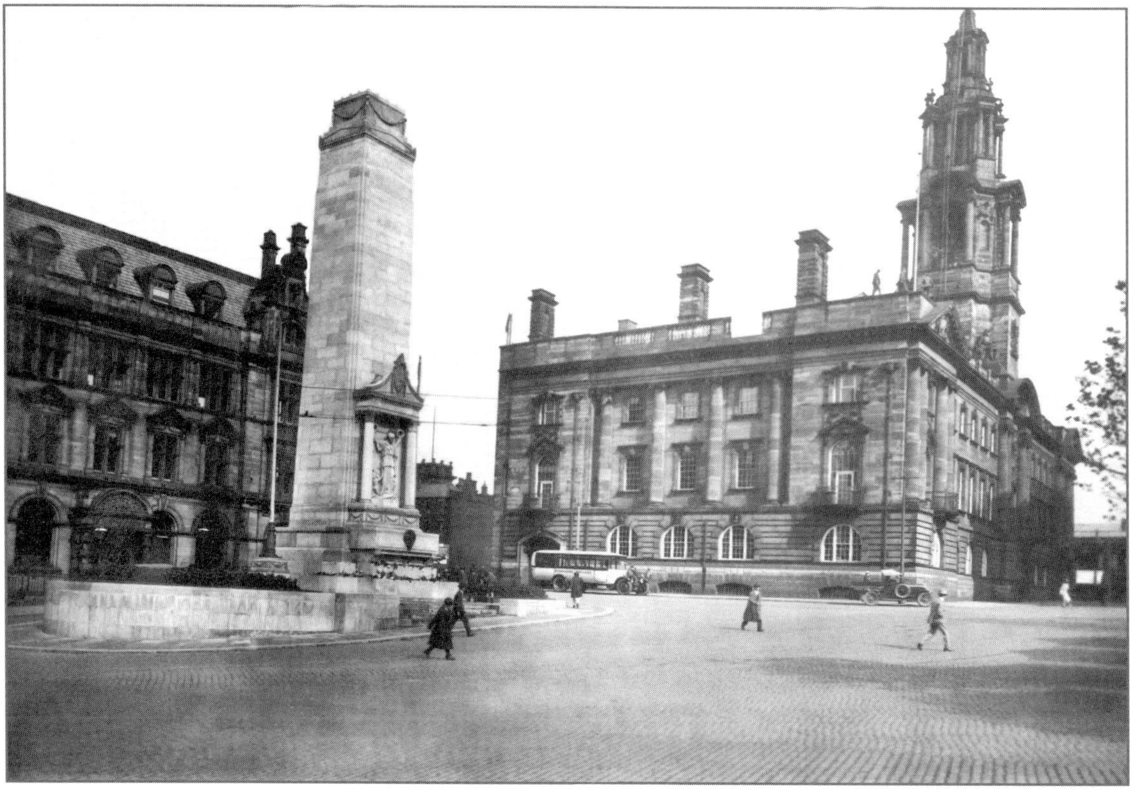

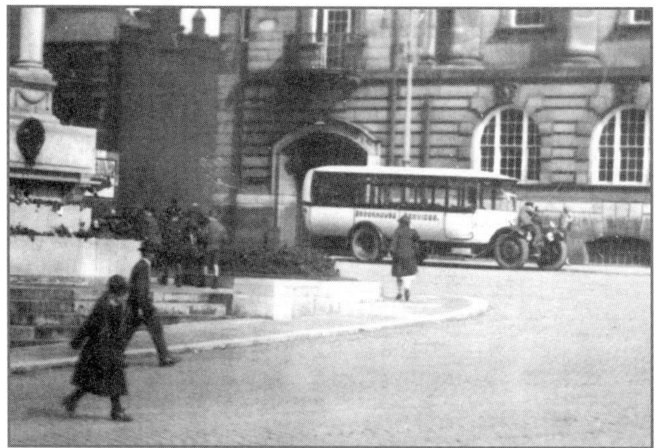

The War Memorial 1926 79110
Preston's War Memorial to those who gave their lives in the Great War had just been erected at this time. The original unveiling date in May 1926 had to be postponed because of the General Strike. There had been a Boer War memorial on this site before this, but it was moved to Avenham Park. You can see it in some of our earlier photographs.

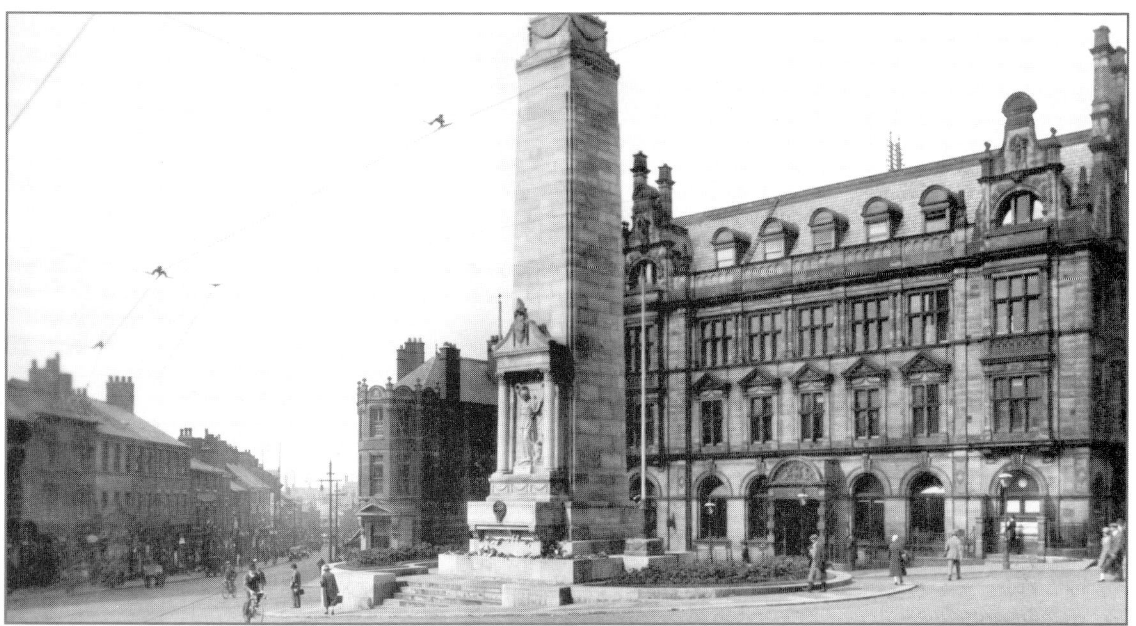

The War Memorial and Friargate 1926 79113
This is a good view of the Great War Memorial which was unveiled in 1926. We can see quite clearly the panel at the front with a helmeted woman holding garlands of victory aloft, with a writhing figure (War) at her feet. To the left we can see down Friargate. The friary of Grey Friars was just to the left of the bottom of the street. Friargate was the second street in Preston to develop shops, and is still a busy shopping area.

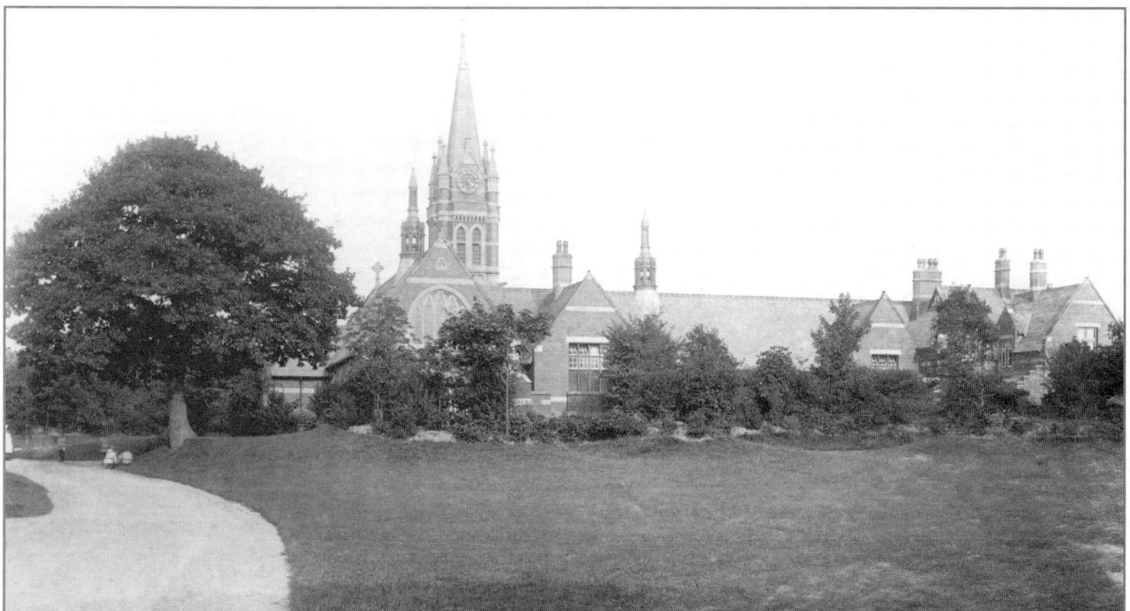

The Harris Orphanage 1893 33099
Preston owes many of its fine buildings to Edmund Harris and his bequests to the town. The trustees did fine work; they made sure that the buildings put up in his name were built with only the best materials, and all had a pleasing overall look, many with fine spires and steeples. The Harris Orphanage was a good example. The trustees bought an area called Crow Trees in 1881 for £4,800 and started to build to the design of Benjamin Sykes.

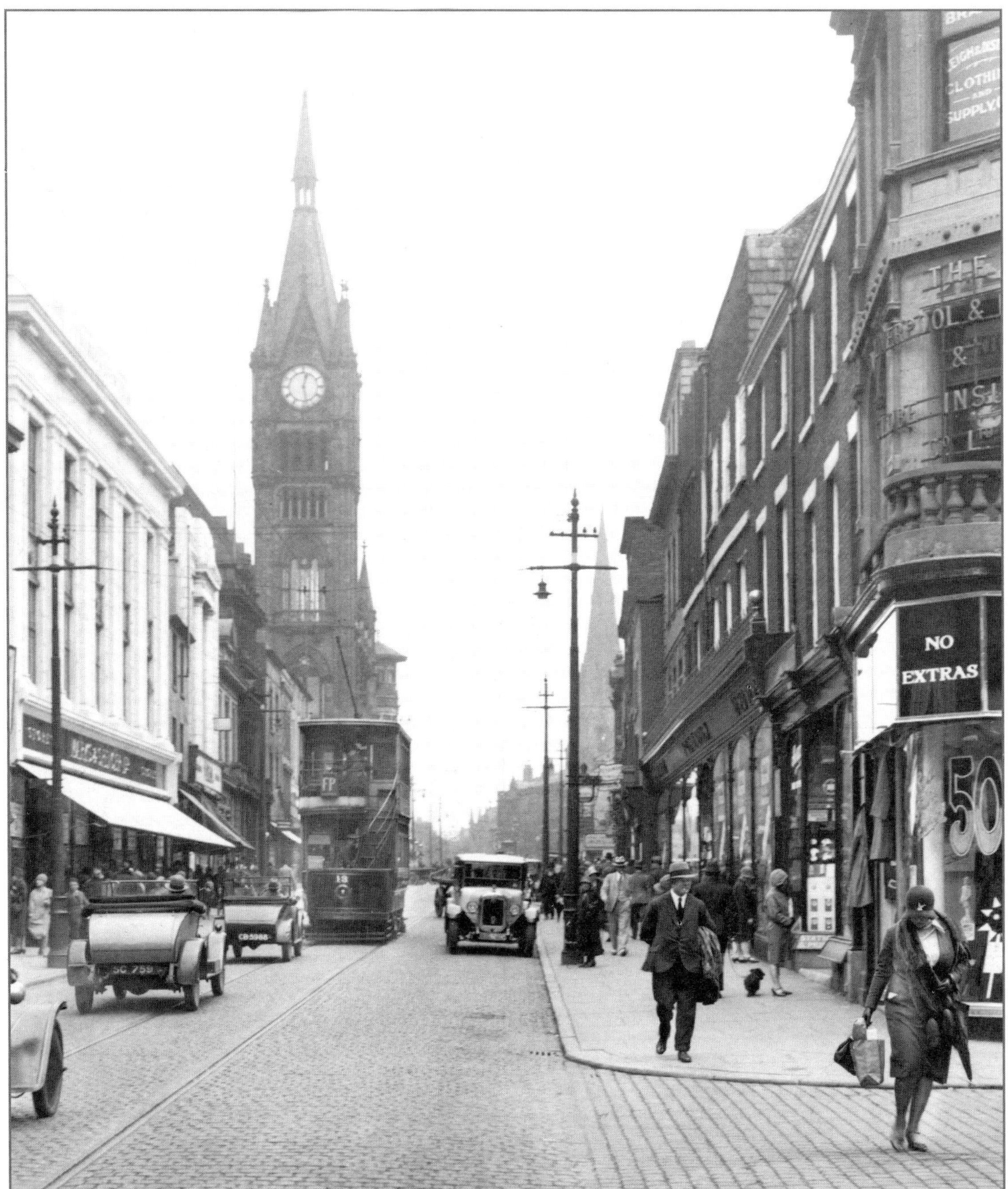

Fishergate 1929 82676

This interesting view was taken in the inter-war years. Because of the narrowness of Fishergate, tram tracks were only single-line in places, and this led to hold-ups and delays at peak periods. Our No 13 tram is passing Marks & Spencer's distinctive building on the left, and some interesting cars are following. As the shops developed at street level, Fishergate became convenient for business offices above, and people visiting the shops could also visit their insurance company or solicitors. The Liverpool, London & Globe Insurance Office is on the right of our picture, and a Coupon Company above. All local insurance companies and companies dealing with the public wanted offices on Fishergate.

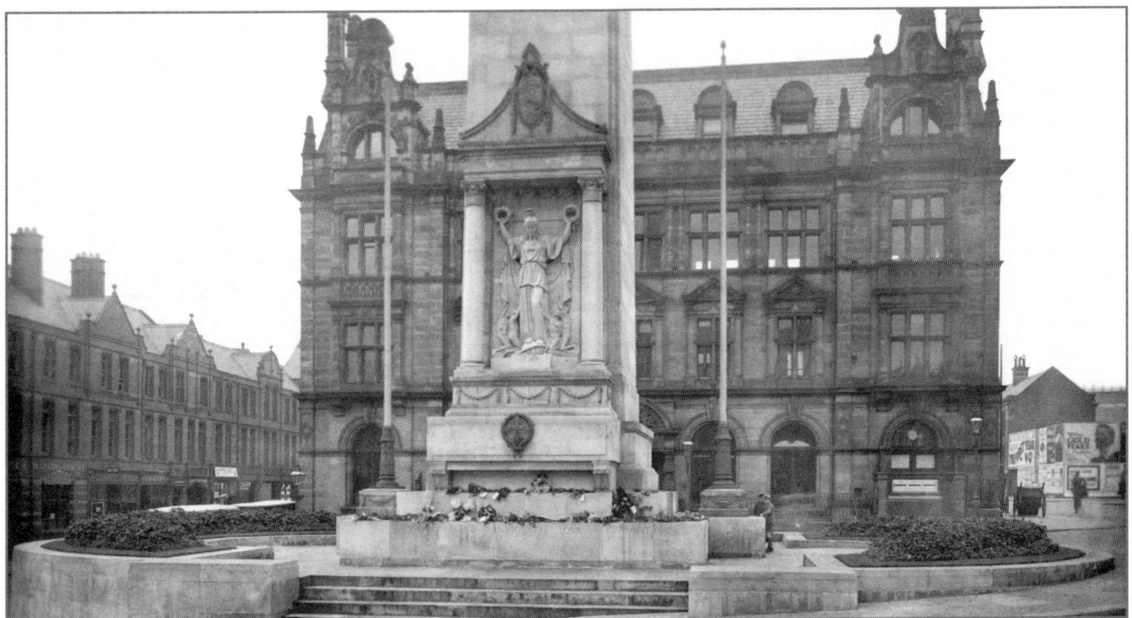

The War Memorial 1926 79115
This fine, solid memorial to those who died in the First World War is shown here in close-up. The Memorial was officially unveiled by Earl Jellicoe on 13 June 1926. It was designed by the grandson of Sir Gilbert Scott, who had designed Preston Town Hall. He included a garden area and a surround, seen clearly here, to keep the area slightly cut-off and special.

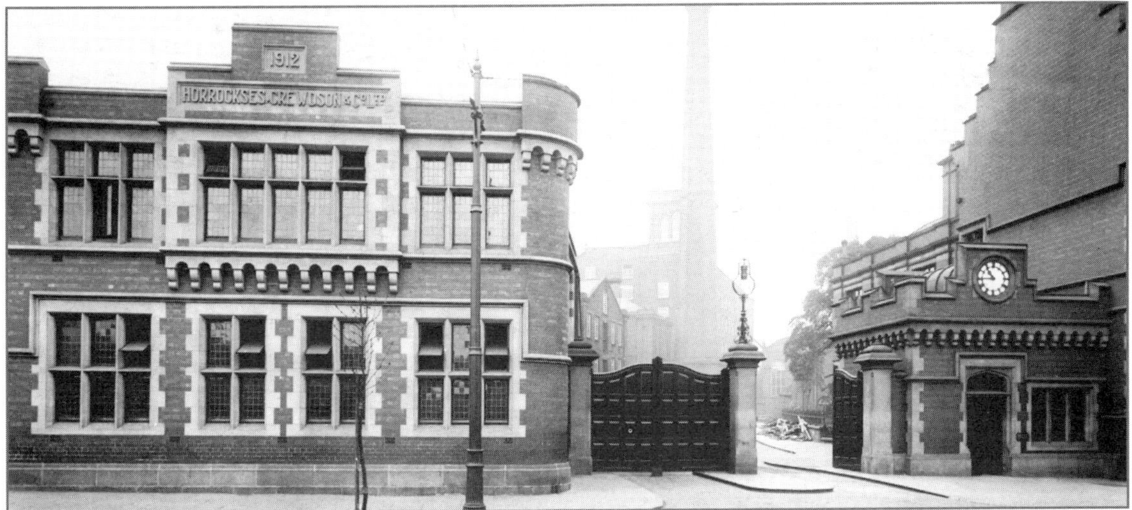

Horrockses, Crewdson & Co Ltd 1913 65593
Here we see the offices and entrance gates of Horrockses, Crewdson & Co on Stanley Street. These gates were built in 1912, the same year that the company was renamed - it was previously John Horrocks'. At the back of this picture are the old works, which date from 1791. John Horrocks was a Preston success, and was always held up as a shining example of man's ingenuity. He arrived in Preston in 1791 from Edgworth, near Bolton. With no real capital, he set to work as a muslin weaver in Turk's Head Court, off Church Street. He put out work for hand-loom weavers, and within a year he had built a factory of his own. Within ten years he had six factories and a house in Golden Square. He had also built Penwortham Lodge, fought a local election, and been elected Member of Parliament. The company he founded became the one we see above.

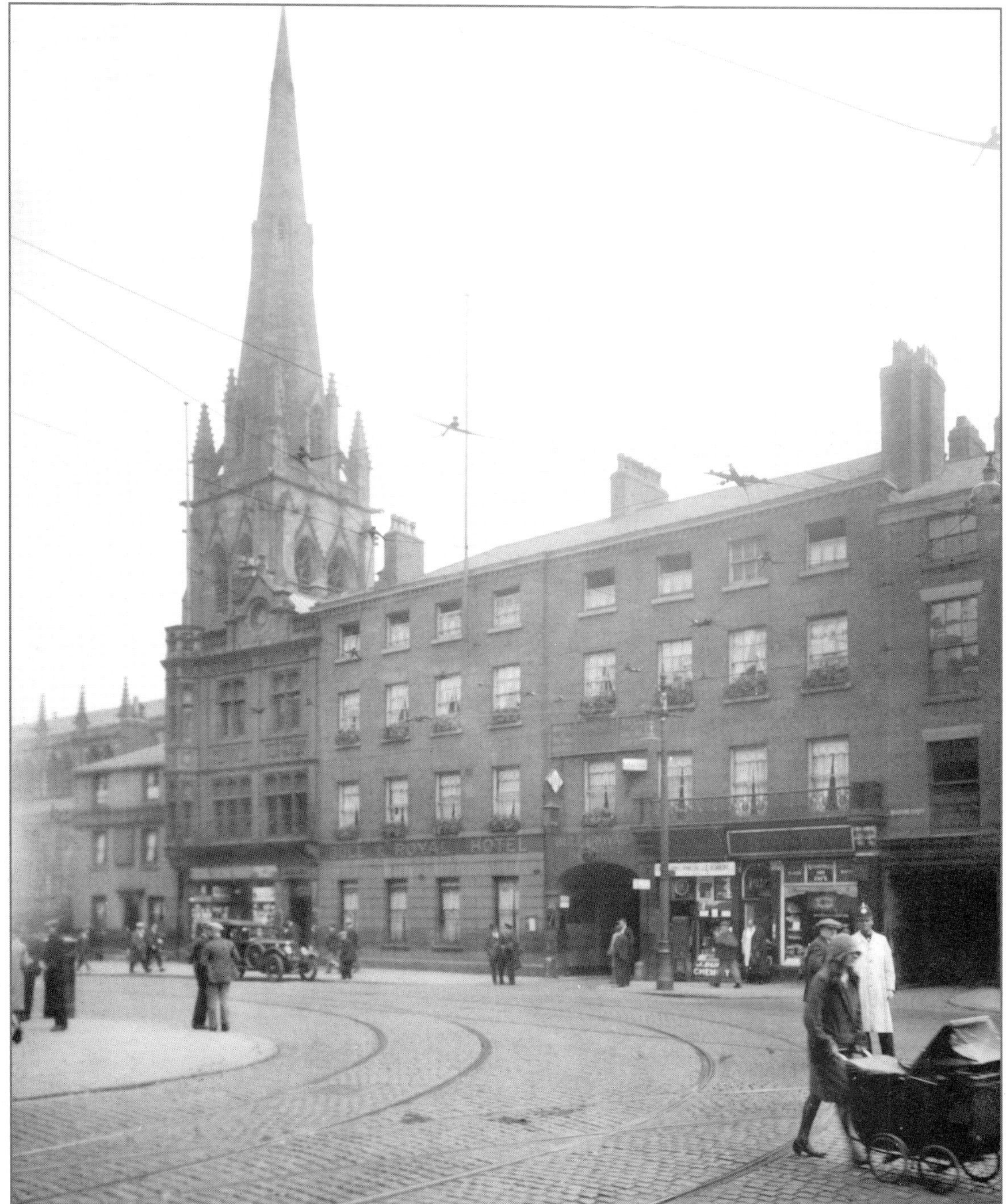

Church Street 1929 82677

Preston Parish Church is now dedicated to St John the Divine, who is the patron saint of the Guild Merchants. The spire rises 205ft above the street. The large tower had ten bells. Right in the centre of our photograph is the Bull & Royal Hotel, one of Preston's most historic hostelries. The part on the left started life as the White Bull, and can be traced back to the mid 1500s. It was here in 1745 that Bonnie Prince Charlie gave a locket containing a portrait of himself to young Miss Pender. It can be seen today in the Harris Museum. The White Bull took in the Royal Hotel next door, and the Bull & Royal was born. Today the hotel has been turned into student accommodation.

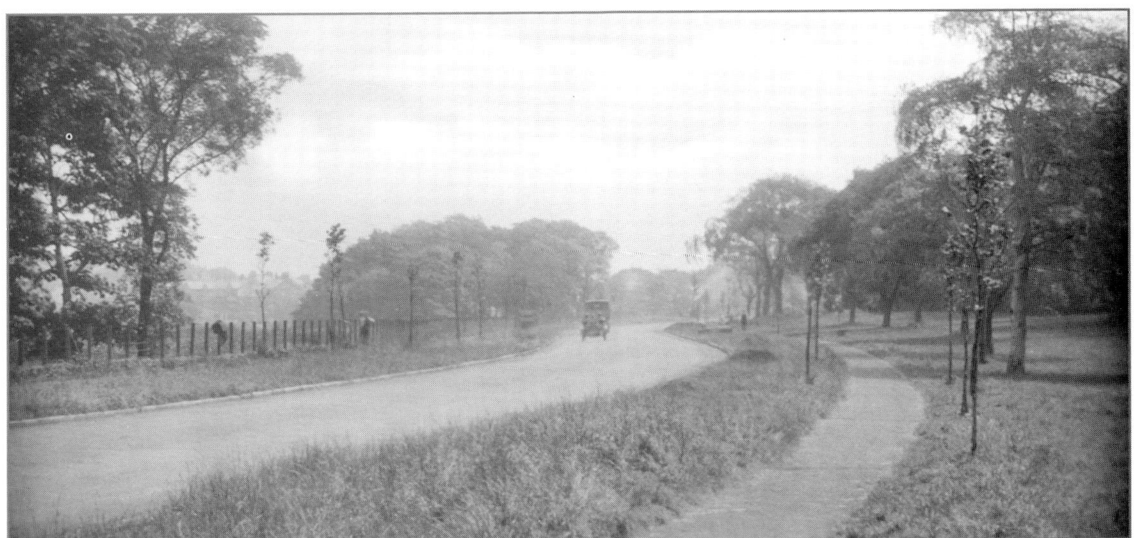

New Road 1924 75839
Preston was always a town that you had to pass through to go north to south, but as the popularity of Blackpool increased, so did the traffic east to west. Liverpool and Manchester both sent traffic over the Ribble bridges and into the dock area to join roads that were full already. After the First World War, it was decided to build a relief road north of the town: that is what we can see here, just after its completion. The housing estates and shops which line the road today are still to come - our view shows an almost empty Blackpool Road in the Deepdale area of Preston. Oh! the hours I have sat in traffic jams on this road in the 1970s and 1980s! To see it new and empty fills me with nostalgia.

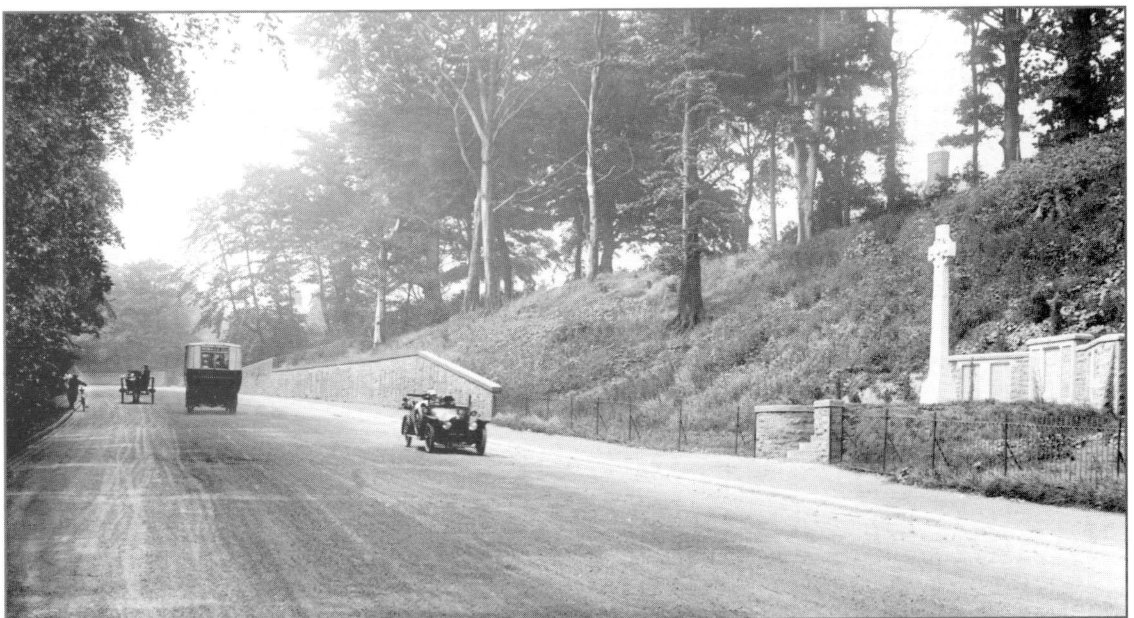

Penwortham Hill 1921 70736
This view shows Penwortham Hill and the climb out of Preston on the Liverpool/Southport road. The newly-erected Penwortham War Memorial is on the right. Note the jaunty open-top car, no doubt heading through Preston and on to Blackpool. There are four modes of transport captured in this photograph - bicycle, horse-drawn carriage, omnibus and car.

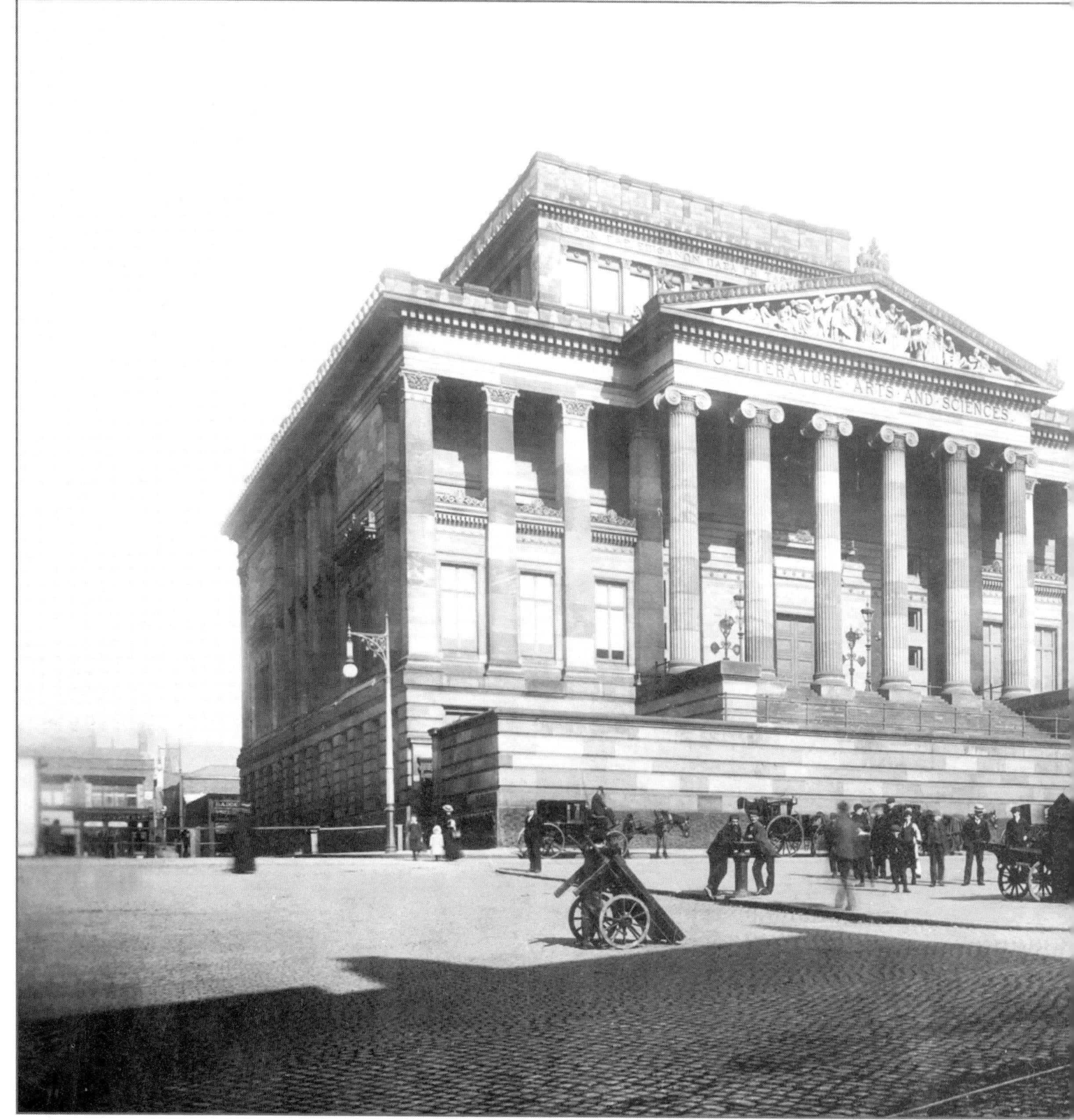

The Harris Library and Art Gallery 1903 50083

Here we see the diamond in the crown that is the centre of Preton. After Edmund Harris died in 1877, plans were put in place, for this magnificent public building built in honour of the Harris family. The Harris family provided the money for the building, and Preston Corporation gave the land; work started in 1881. The foundation stone was laid in Guild Week 1882 by Lord Lathom. The Library, designed by Preston architect James Hibbert, was opened on 26 October 1893 by Lord Derby, but it was another two years before the Art Gallery was ready to open. 'To Literature Arts and Sciences' is carved above the classical Greek-style entrance. On the other three sides of the building are carved the following inscriptions: 'The Mental Riches You May Here Acquire, Abide With You Always', 'On Earth There Is Nothing Greater Than Man. In Men There Is Nothing Great But Mind', and 'Reverence In Man, That Which Is Supreme'. These timeless words give food for thought in today's busy world.

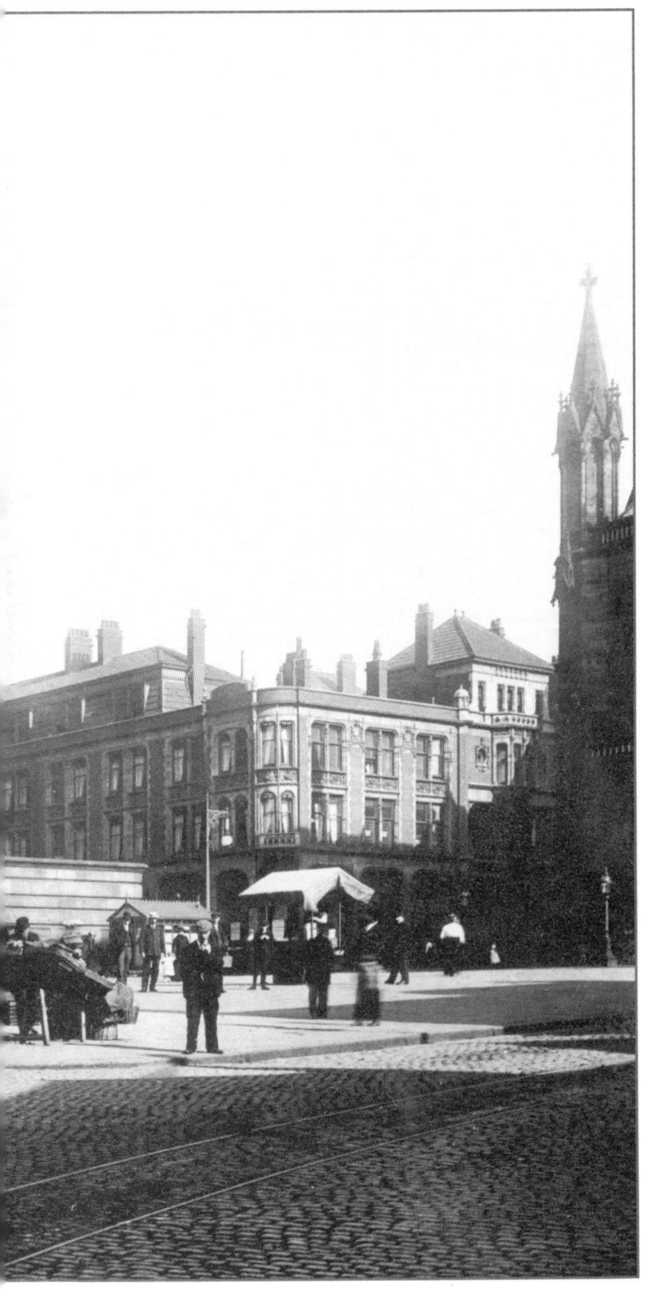

The Buildings of Preston

Preston is a fine town - and it looks a fine town. Because so many of its grand Victorian buildings remain, and because it has managed to keep some of its older squares intact, it retains small areas of peace amidst the bustle of everyday life. The more you travel to other towns and cities in Great Britain, the more you appreciate Market Square for its imposing buildings, its open space and its various uses. Winckley Square has history in every building, and it is a gem in itself. It is a shame that Preston Grammar School was pulled down so quickly, and there are other buildings that should have had a little more consideration, but that was the mood of the 1960s - 'clear it away, think of today'. As I write now, a fierce debate is going on over Preston Bus Station, built in the 1960s around Tithebarn Street. It really does personify the late 1960s and the stark concrete architectural style of the time. I know 1960 is only forty years or so ago, but it would be nice if this Bus Station was given listed status and was saved. Many people would like to remind town planners that everything should not just be swept away.

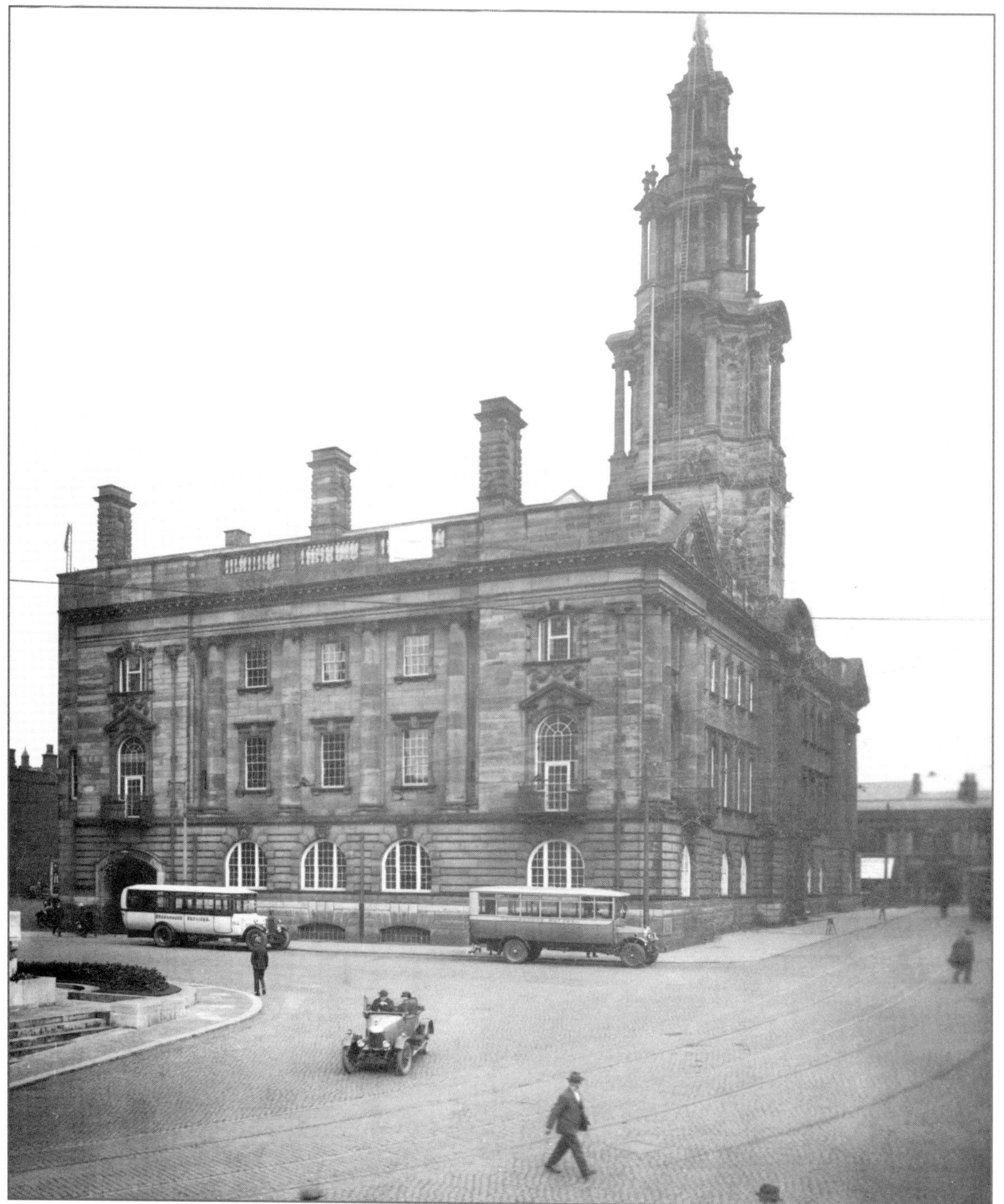

The County Sessions House 1926 79111

Designed by H Littler, the County Architect, in 1890 and built in 1900, the County Sessions House stands in Market Square. It was built at a cost of £90,000, which included buying the site. The design is English Renaissance; the tower looks like a wedding cake, with layer on layer climbing 179ft high into the sky. There were two courts when it opened, both furnished in oak, and situated either side of an Assembly Hall. There was also a Grand Jury Room, a Judge's Room, a Solicitors' Room and a Grand Dining Room. Before this was built, the court met at the Old Court House (built in 1827) next to the prison at the bottom of Church Street.

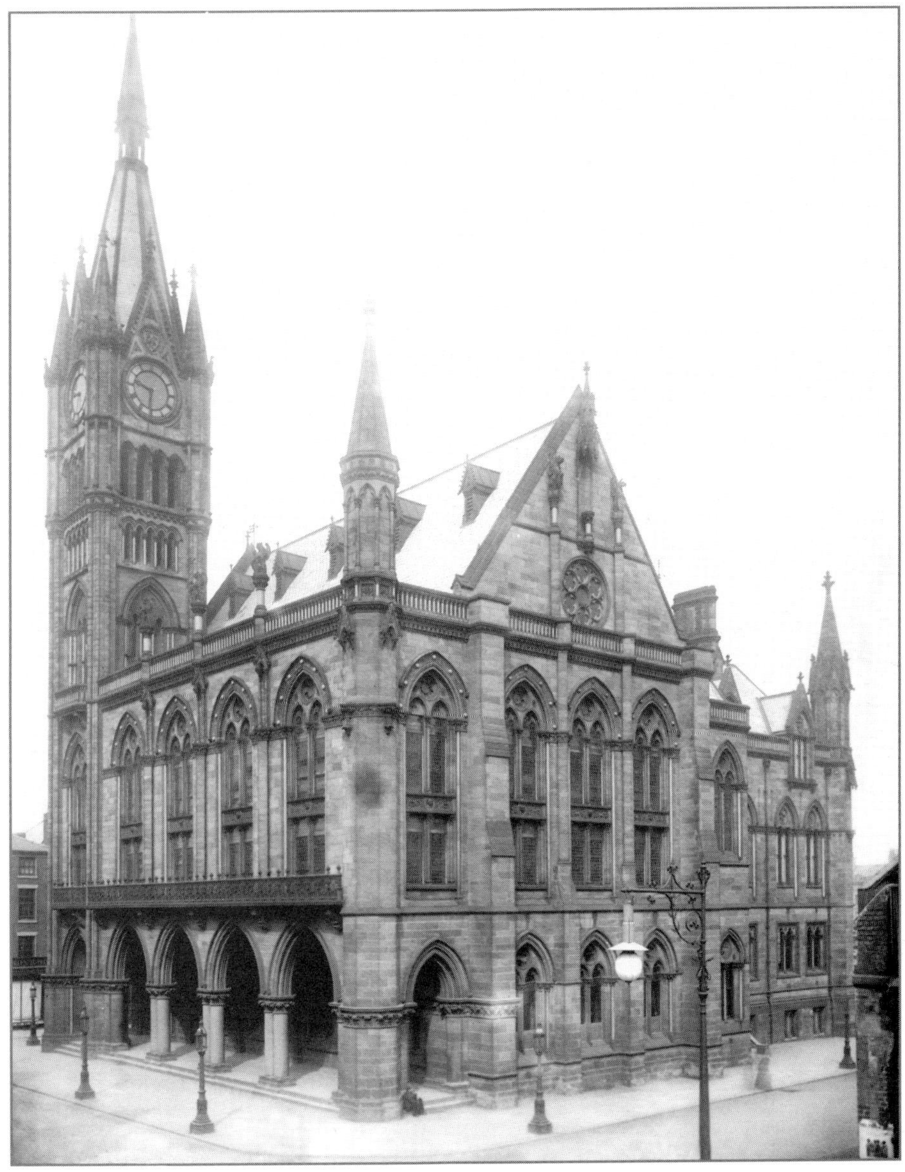

The Town Hall 1893 33086

This photograph was taken from Church Street. At the Town Hall, Fishergate becomes Church Street with no other demarcation than that one has passed this fine building. The building was designed by Sir Gilbert Scott, and the foundation stone was laid with full masonic honours during Guild Week in September 1862. Excursion trains brought fellow masons from every town and city in Lancashire to join in the celebration. There was a great debate about the position of the building, and about which way it should face. Although our photograph has captured the tower and frontages well, the passers-by could not really appreciate it from the close confines of Church Street and Fishergate. Even Gilbert Scott was drawn into the debate, but he sent a letter to the council which said 'such a fine building will look good anywhere', and thus got himself off the hook. On 14 March 1947, the alarm went up that the town hall was on fire. Fire appliances fought until the next morning to put out the flames, but by then the building stood completely gutted. Ten fire-fighting units had fought through the night. The four-and-a-half ton bell of the clock tower fell right down the tower, and could be heard 'sounding' as falling masonry hit it. There were plans to re-build or save part of the building, but it was cleared away in 1962. The offices there today were finished in 1964.

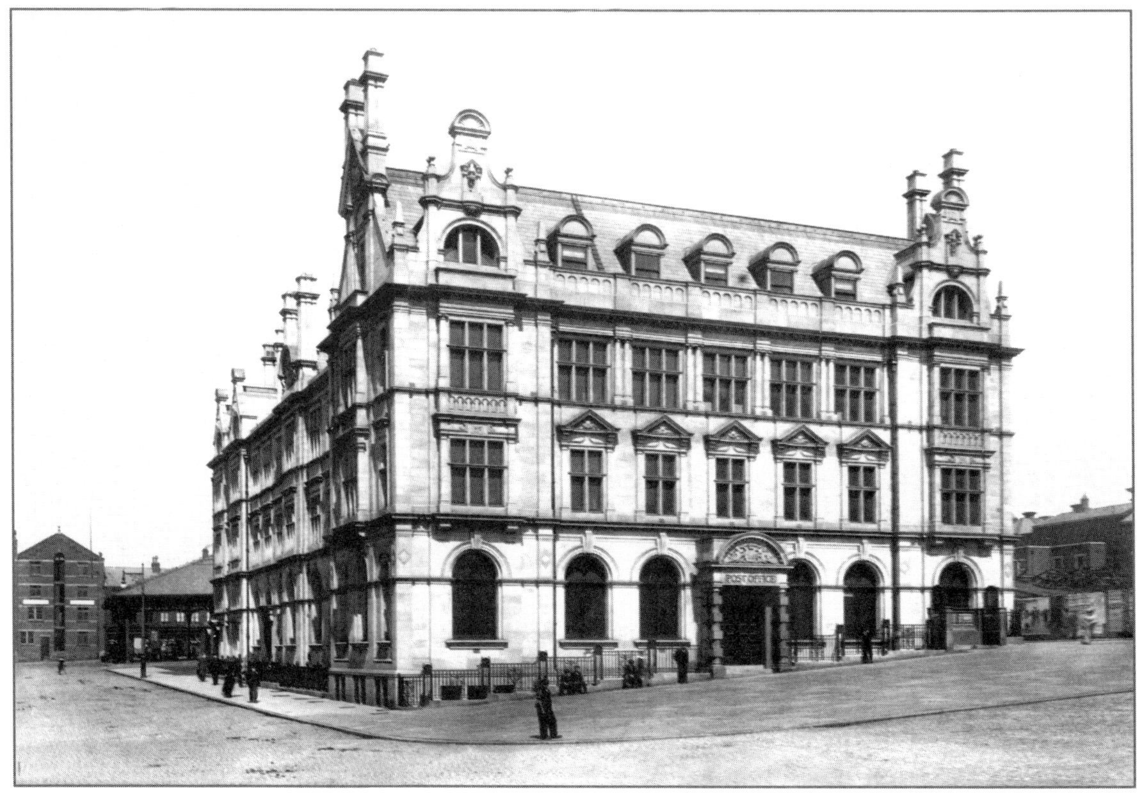

The New Post Office 1903 50085
Here we see Preston Post Office just a couple of years after it opened. The original Preston Post Office had been at the south end of Wide Shambles in a building leaning on the side of the shambles. When this much-needed new Post Office was built, to make it look more impressive it was faced with stone from Storeton Quarry in the Wirral. After opening, one of its first duties was to produce a special frank for the post, just for the 1902 Guild celebrations. The Post Office was open from 7.30am to 7.30pm most days, and open all day Saturday as well. This photograph it was taken before the Boer War Memorial and Gardens were erected.

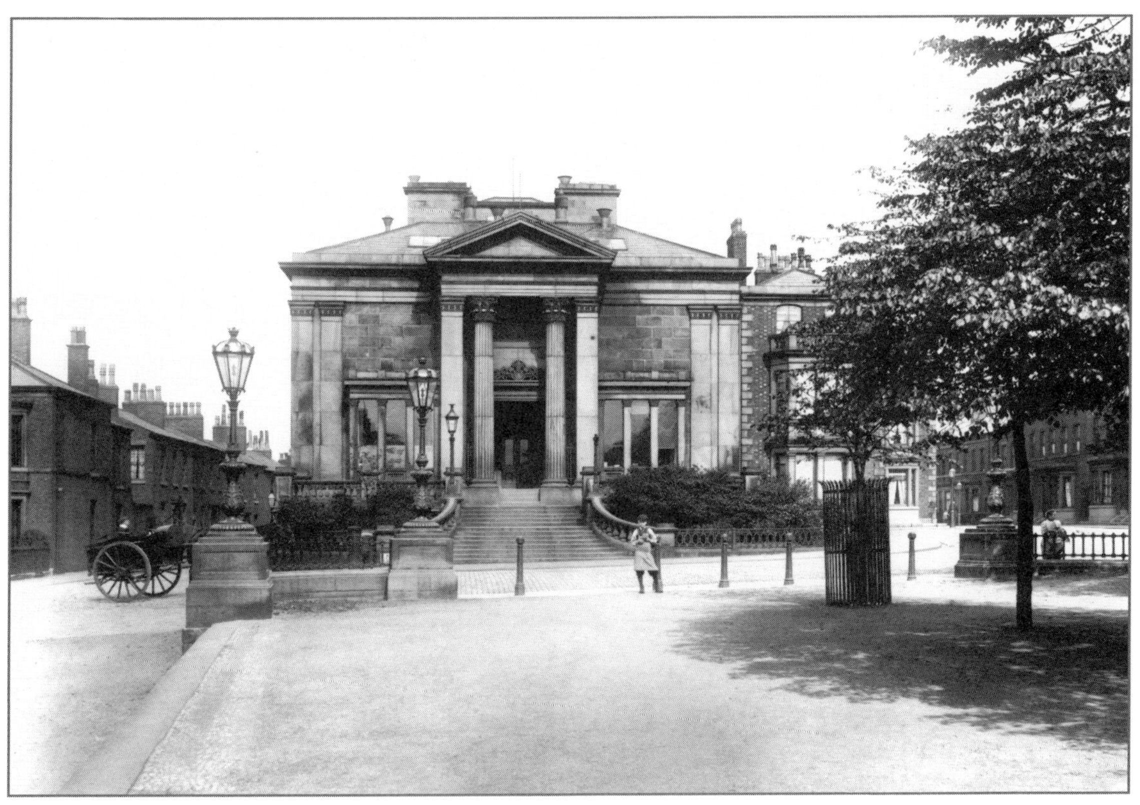

The Harris Institute 1903 50071

This building started life as The Institute for the Diffusion of Knowledge, a movement that was very popular at the time Victoria ascended to the throne. It opened in October 1850, built to a design by local architect John Welsh. By 1882, the building was run-down; it was then that the Trustees of the Harris Estates gave £40,000 for its restoration. On the right of the building is an extension, designed by the architect James Hibbert, and this was the Chemistry and Physics Laboratories. The Institute quickly established itself, and was very popular. By the time of our photograph, about 5,000 students had passed through its portals. In 1932 the laboratories were moved out, and the building became a School of Art, known locally as the Art College. It became part of Harris College in 1956, Preston Polytechnic in 1973 and the University of Central Lancashire in 1992.

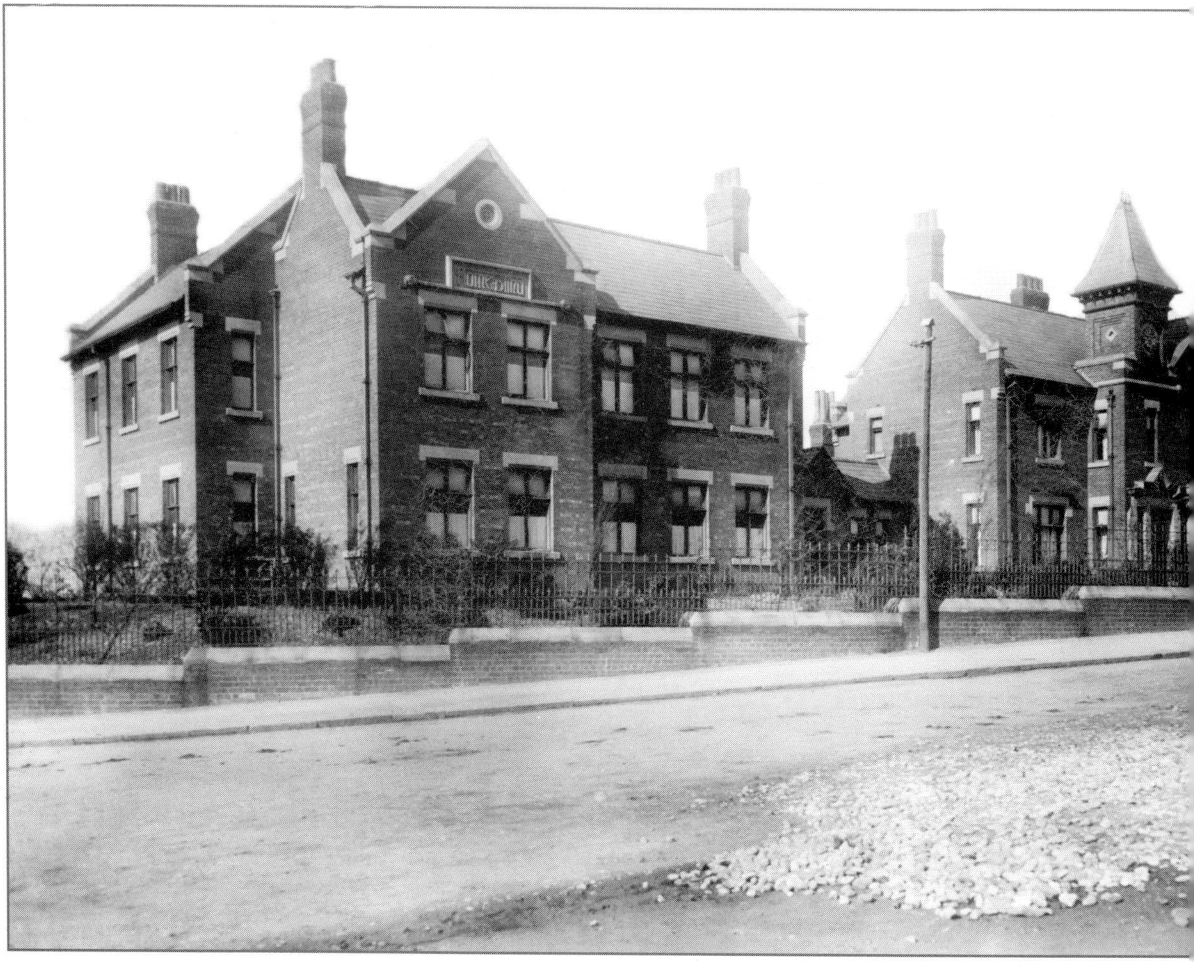

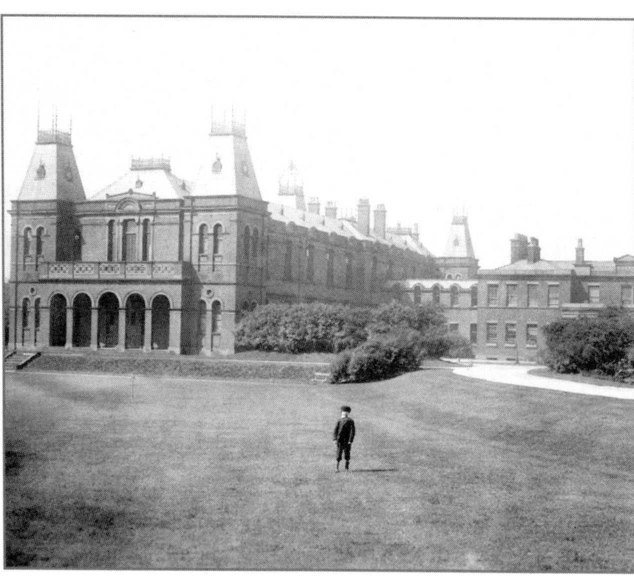

◄ **The Infirmary 1894** 34384

The Infirmary was opened in 1870, funded with the money left by Edmund Harris, and in 1884 a Children's Ward had been opened. One of the consultants at the time of our photograph was Sir Charles Brown (1836-1926). Dr Charles Brown was noted for putting his hand in his own pocket if the Hospital had need of any new equipment, especially for the Children's Ward. He was made Medical Officer for Preston in 1870, and in 1905 he paid for a new Operating Theatre to be built at the hospital. This grand gentleman did not retire from service to the Infirmary until 1922, when he was aged 86. As part of Queen Victoria's Diamond Jubilee Honours, the Infirmary was given a royal prefix. It was going to be the Royal Infirmary, Preston, but someone noticed that the initials would have been R I P, so it became Preston Royal Infirmary. The Royal title was removed in 1982, and today it is a hall of residence for students.

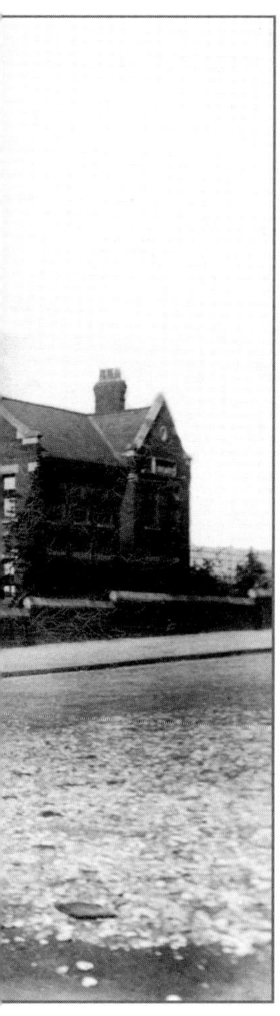

◄ **The Home for the Blind 1897** 40999

A workshop for the blind opened in the mid 1850s in a cottage in North Road. In 1866 the Derby School for the Blind was founded, and named in honour of Lord Derby in recognition of his support. In 1893 a site at Fulwood was bought and the fine solid Victorian building we see here was started. The foundation stone was laid on 30 September 1893 by Lady Derby. The school closed in 1987, and the building was turned into offices.

▼ **The Harris Orphanage 1893** 33098

The Harris Orphanage opened in 1888 after £100,000 was set aside by the Trustees of the Harris Estate to build and equip such an establishment. Local architect Benjamin Sykes designed the building in domestic Gothic style. At the time of this photograph, there were about one hundred and sixty children resident here. The school was run on the 'group' system (unusual then, and very advanced for the time): the children lived in groups and learnt how to look after one another like a large family. At the age of fifteen the young adults were launched into the real world, or returned to any relatives that could be found. The Orphanage had a gymnasium, swimming baths, a hospital, workshops and a chapel, so every care was given to its charges. In 1914 Clayton Hall was built in the grounds to give added leisure facilities; it cost £2,000. In 1948 the building became Fulwood and Caldy Comprehensive School, which later merged with Ingol and Lightfoot Primary School to become the Harris County Primary School.

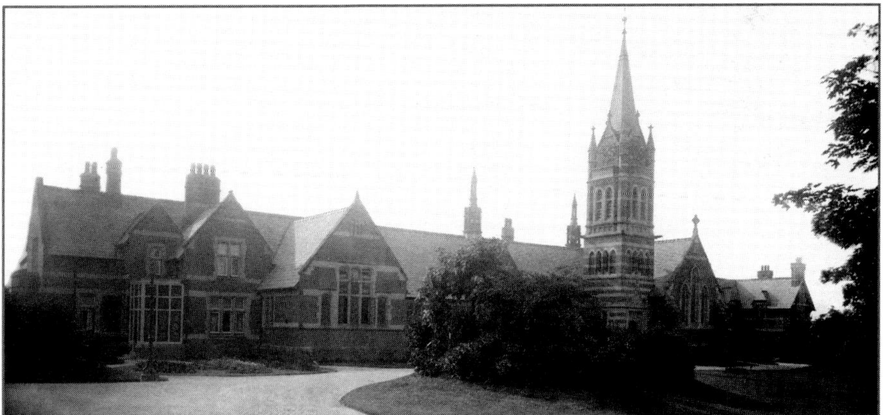

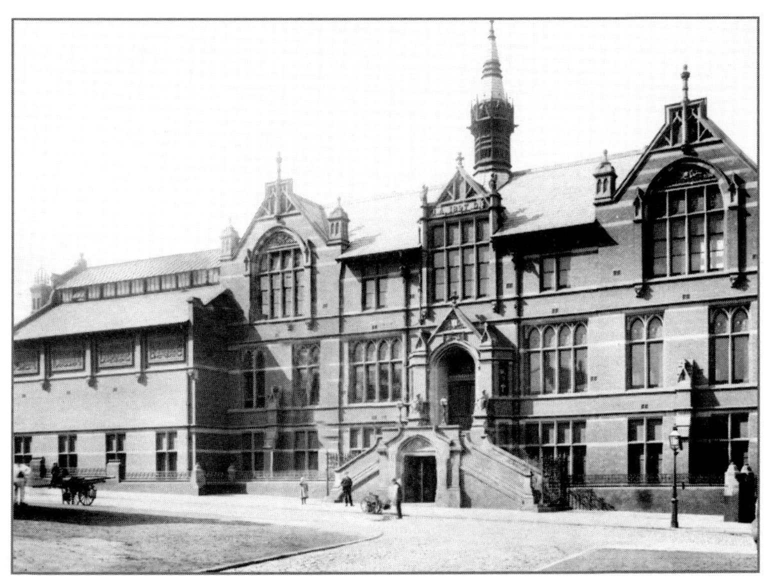

◄ **The Technical School 1903** 50070

The foundation stone of the Victoria Jubilee Technical School was laid in July 1895; the purpose of the School was to give relief to the over-full Harris Institute. The School was declared open by the Countess of Derby in September 1897, and was an immediate success. Many of the classes and facilities were connected to local industries, and there was a whole department for training for the cotton industry. There was a warping and winding room, and a weaving shed with eighty hand looms and twenty power looms. The school developed facilities for teaching electrical skills, and an Electrical Engineering Laboratory was added in Edwardian times. The building has been added to and rebuilt, and is now part of the University of Central Lancashire.

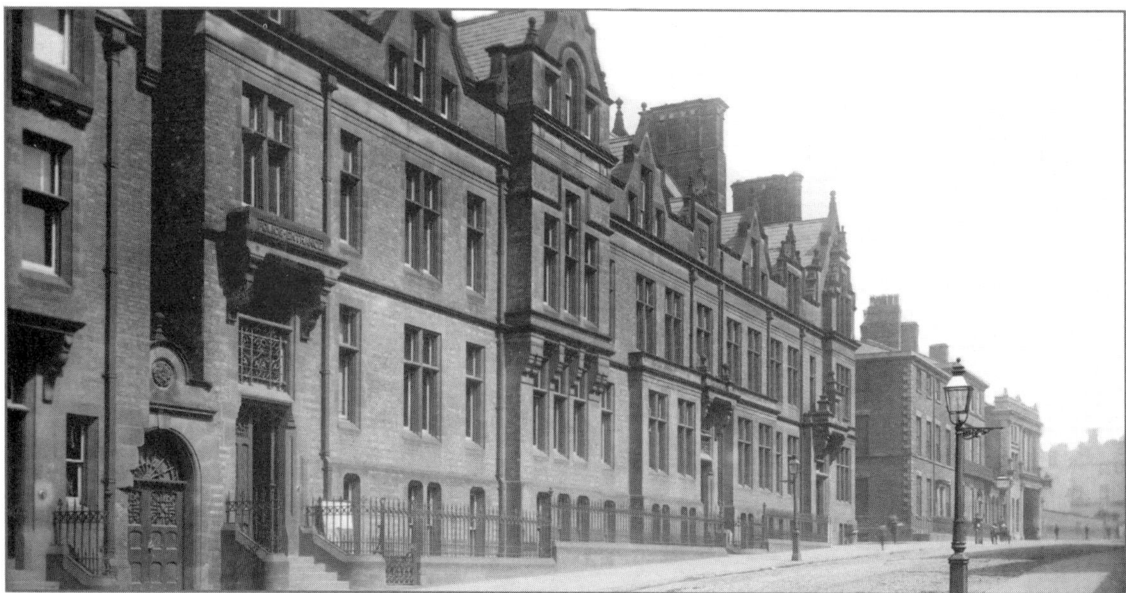

County Hall 1894 34385
Preston is a County Borough, and County Hall was built in 1882 to run and administer the borough. The County Magistrates' Court ran on simple and firm sets of rules, relying on moral and ethical principles as much as on legislature. Because of the work of the county council the building soon became too small, and in 1930 the council were occupying no less than seven other buildings. A further block was built in 1934 (at a cost of £130,000) on Pitt Street and Marchwood Street.

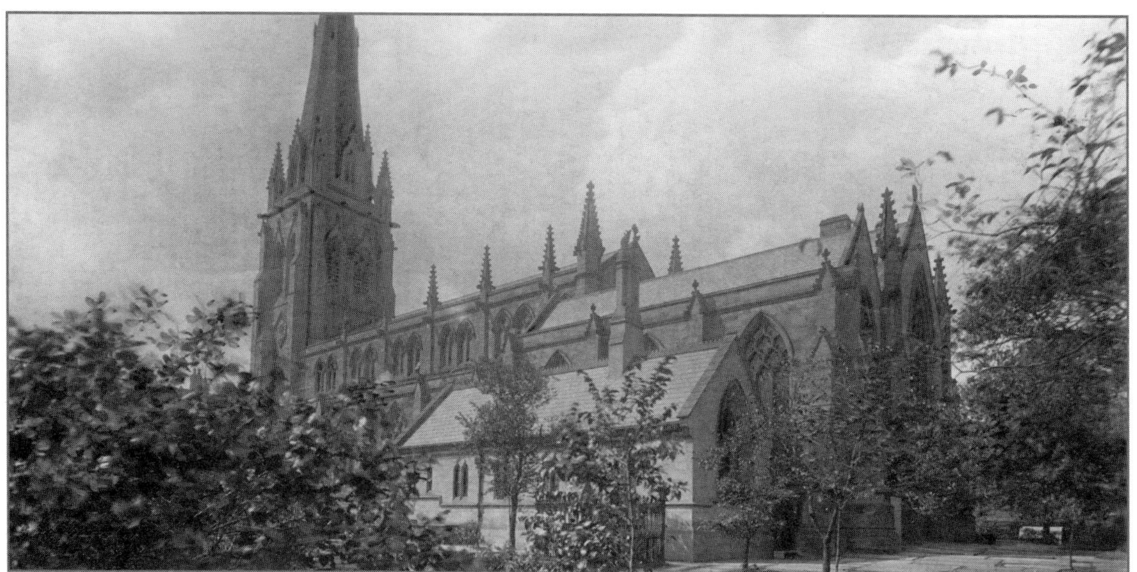

The Parish Church 1893 33088
This unusual view of Preston Parish Church was taken from the back of the church. There has been a church on this site since the 7th century; the first church was dedicated to St Wilfrid. Later on, when the Guilds were established, the dedication was changed to St John the Divine, who was patron saint of the Guild Merchants. The church was rebuilt in 1770 and 1854. In 1855 it was altered and restored at a cost of £9,500, and a further £2,000 was spent in 1885 to improve the church and put in gas fittings. When you enter the church today, you cannot help being impressed with the strong military connections displayed - there are many army memorials to be seen.

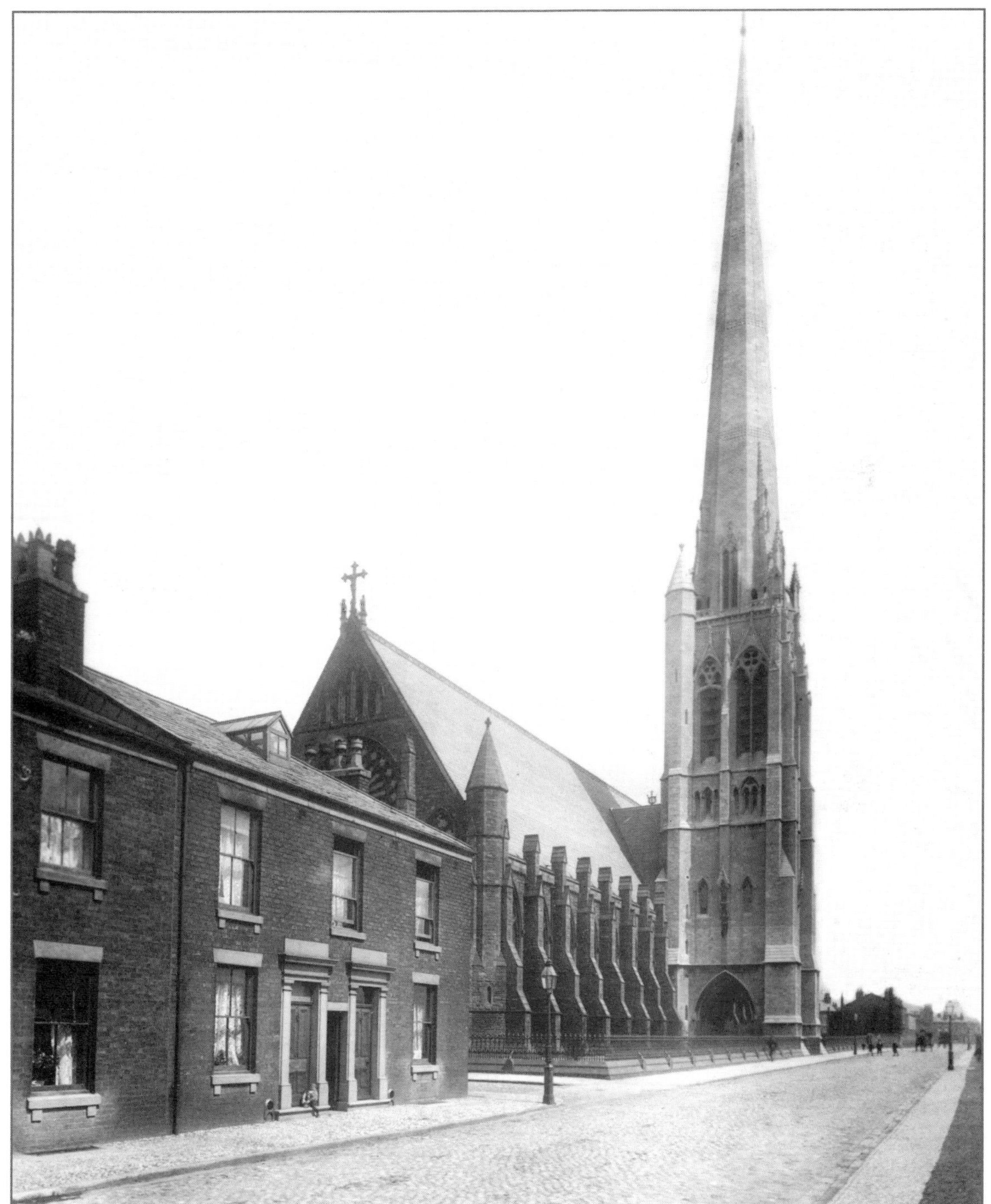

St Walburgh's Church 1897 40996
The spire that towers above everything else in Preston is the 303ft high spire of St Walburgh's Church. The church was built on what was Maudland Bank, and the foundation stone was laid in 1850. Four years later the church opened, but the spire was not added until 1867. This imposing spire was designed by Joseph Aloysius Hansom, who found lasting fame by designing the Hansom cab. Local legend has it that hundreds of railway sleepers hold up the outside fabric of the spire.

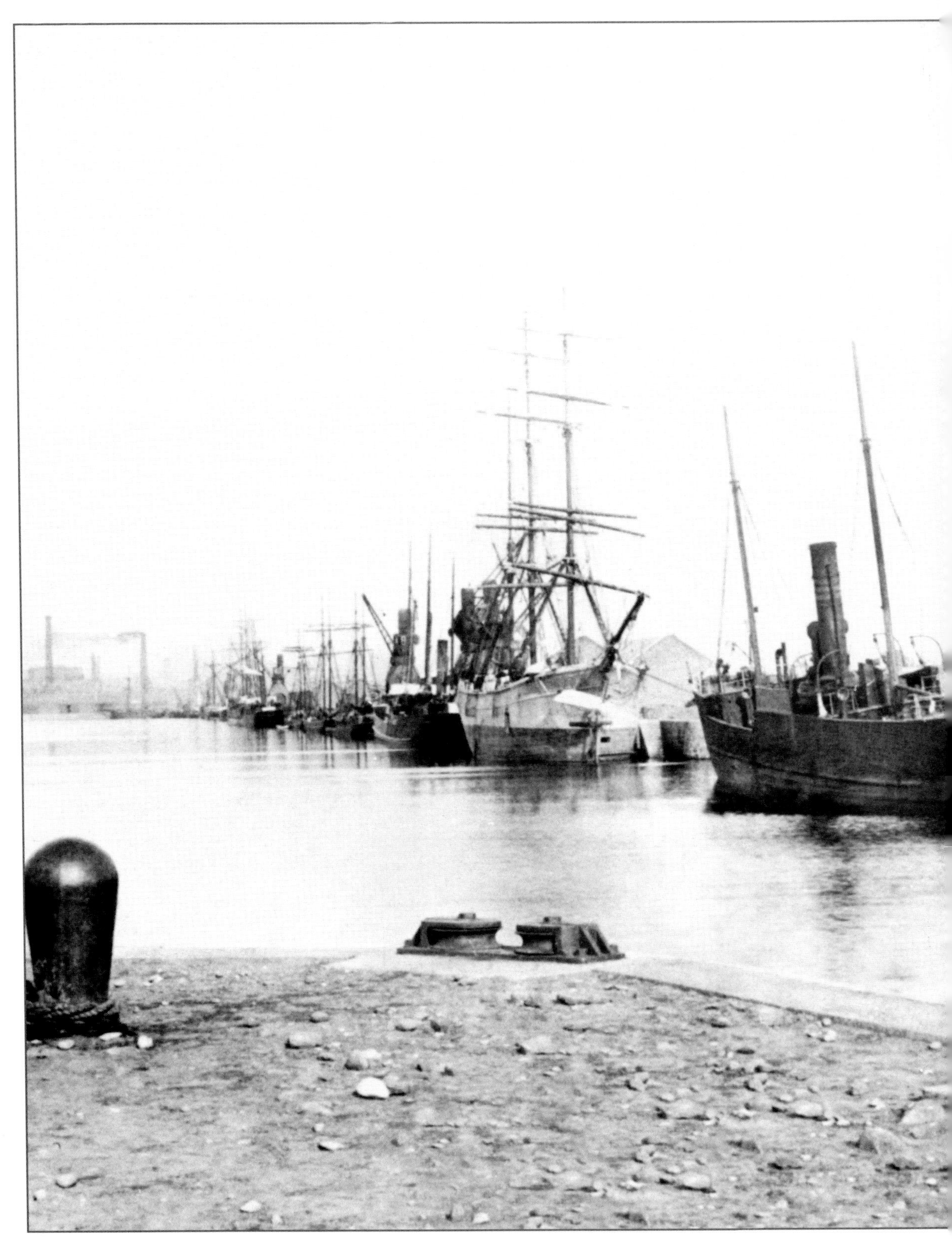

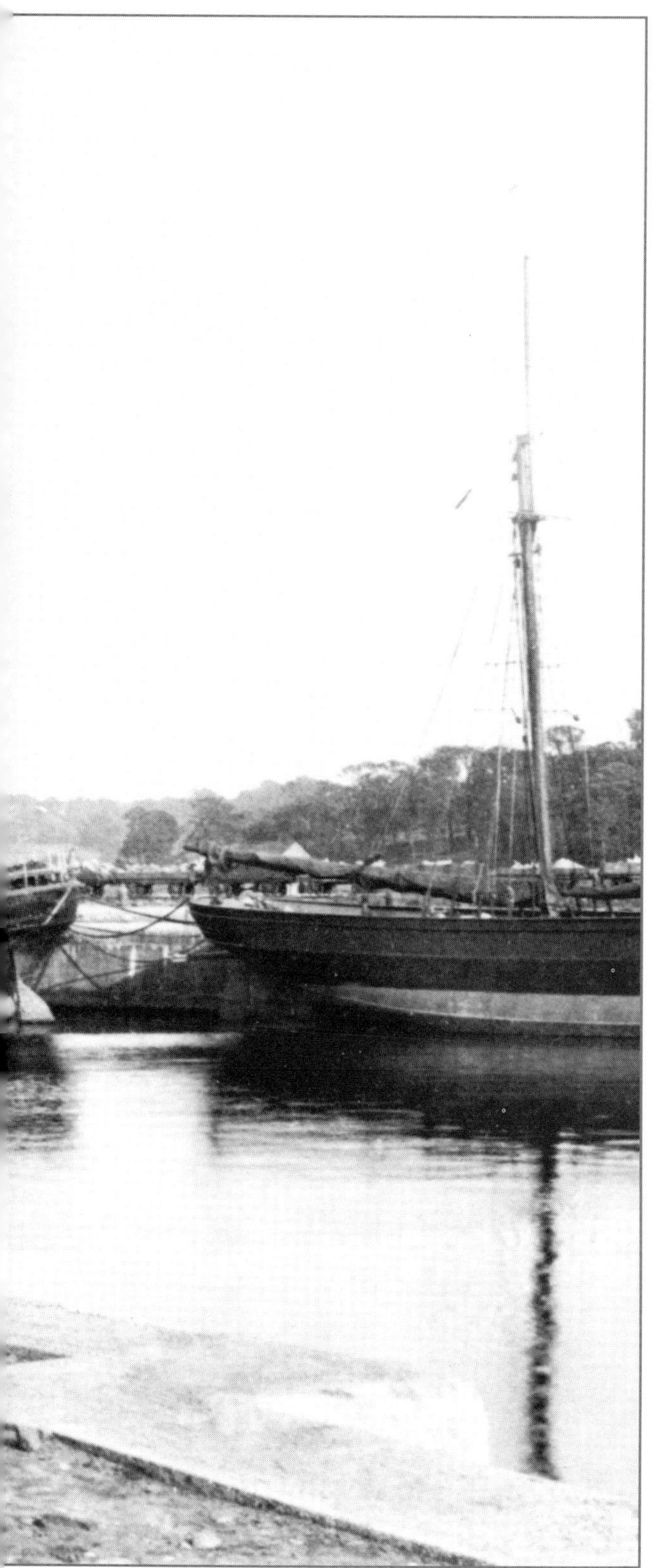

The River Ribble and the Docks

Preston is set on the broad River Ribble, and is near enough to the coast to have been considered a port from early times. In 1841 it was noted that 'extensive improvements are at this time being undertaken to enable ships bigger that one hundred and fifty tons burden to navigate the river to Preston'. A company with £50,000 capital had been formed by Acts of Parliament in 1837 and 1838 to dredge, deepen and straighten the Ribble and bring more trade to the town. River dues paid in 1840 were about £1,000 per annum. The rights of the company, the Ribble Navigation Co, passed to Preston Corporation in 1882, and work started soon after on building docks for the town. These docks opened in 1892, and lasted for fewer than ninety years. The reason was mainly silting and shifting sandbanks, which made navigation difficult along the fourteen miles of the Ribble from Lytham to Preston.

The Docks 1893 33097
This photograph of the docks was taken just a year after they were opened. Here we see the Albert Edward Dock basin, looking from the entrance towards the town. Amongst the cargo which was being unloaded here in our picture would have been timber, flax and china clay.

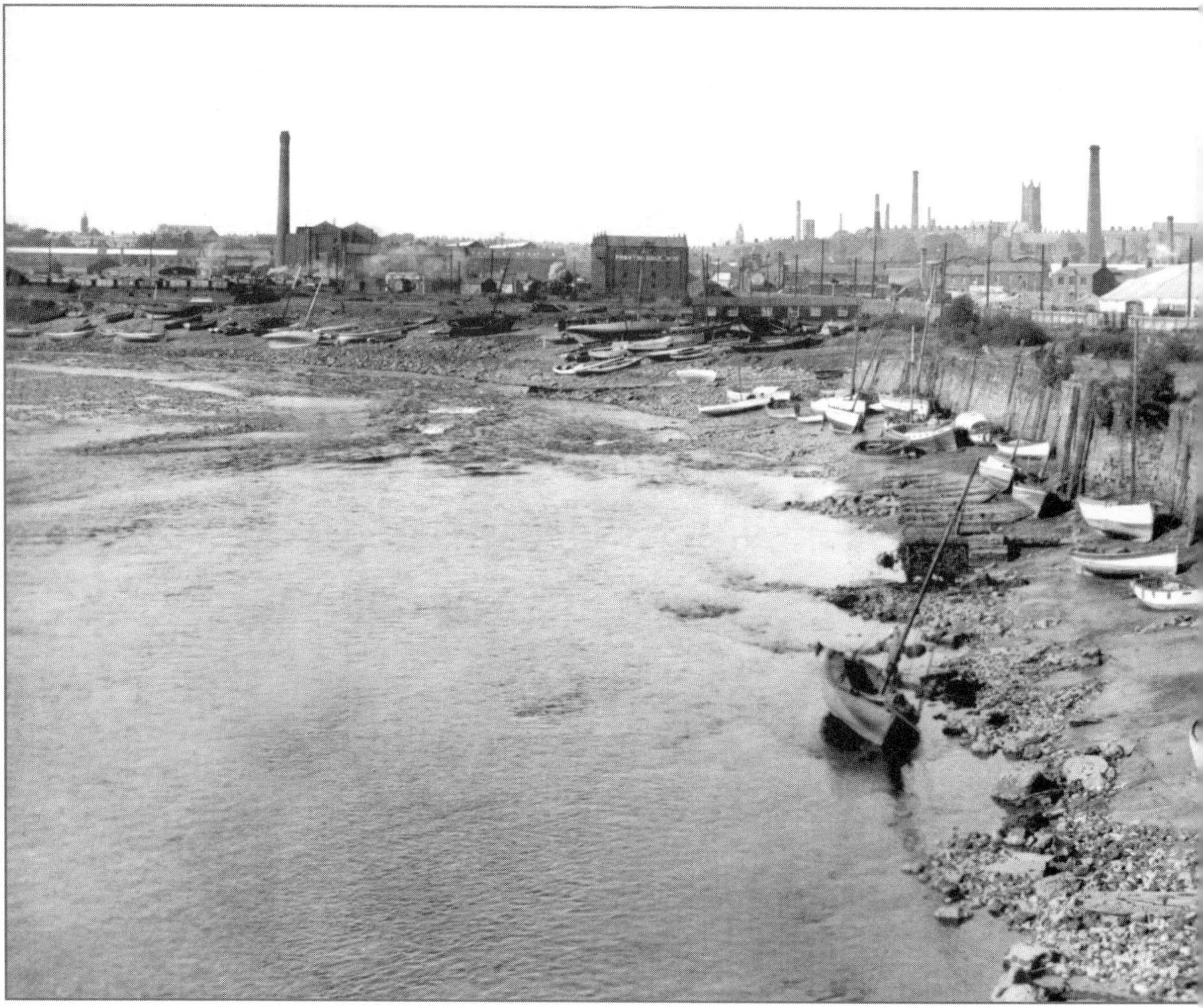

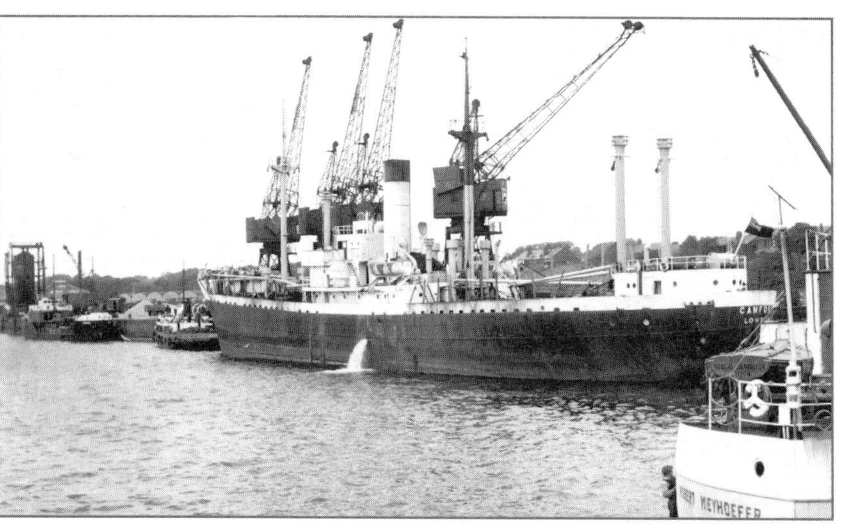

◄ **The Docks c1955** P113033
Although they are referred to as docks, there was really only one dock, the Albert Edward Dock. was named in honour of Queen Victoria's second son, who opened the dock when he was the Duke of Edinburgh. At the time of our picture, vessels of up to 51,000 tons could use the dock, and there was a 21ft draught. Petroleum products were among the imports, as were bananas. The ship in the centre is the 'Canford', registered in London, with a Bremen ship in the right-hand corner.

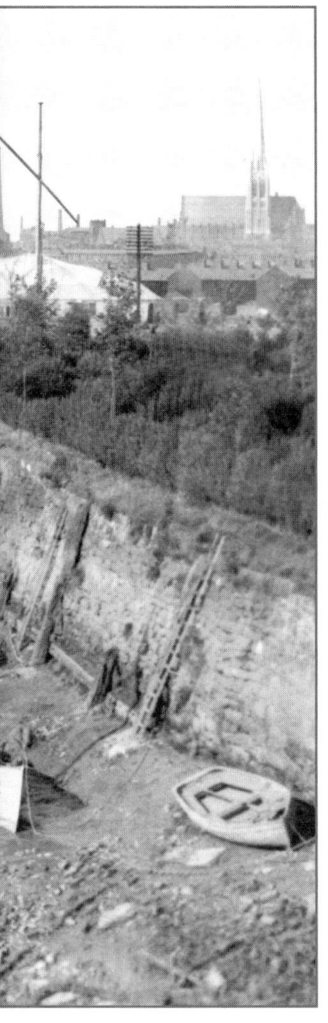

The Ribble 1926 79117

It was this river bank area that had been used as berthing places for small ships carrying flax, which came to the town long before the docks were opened. As we can see, when the tide went out and the river was low nothing much could go on, though some ships could continue to unload once they were tied up. On the skyline you can see the bulk of one of the dock buildings, and the impressive spire of St Walburgh's Church.

The Timber Quay, North Side c1955 P113047

Timber had always been one of Preston's main imports. Even before the docks opened, timber-carrying ships from all over Europe would come into these sheltered waters near Penwortham Hill and unload. Just before the First World War, the port went through a very bad patch owing to shifting sands at the river mouth. The year 1909 saw hardly any but the smallest boats in Preston Docks, and the council had to dig deep into their coffers for dredging work before things started to pick up again.

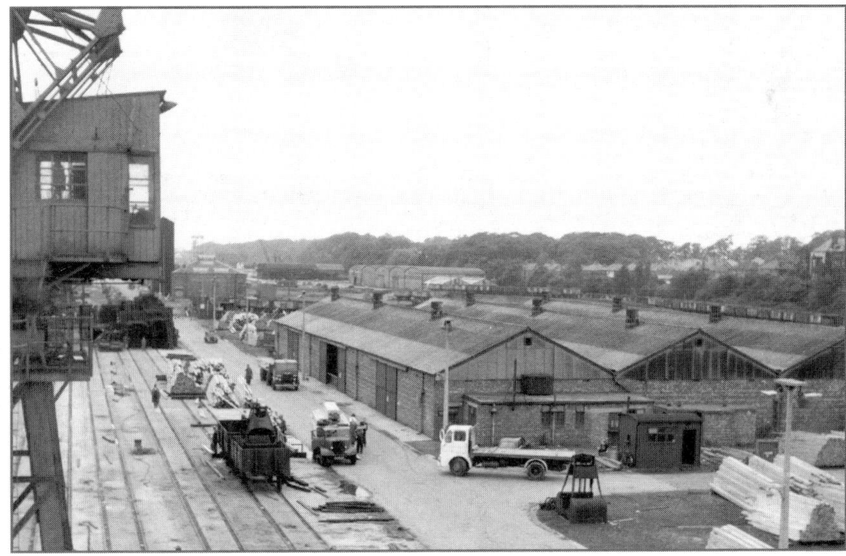

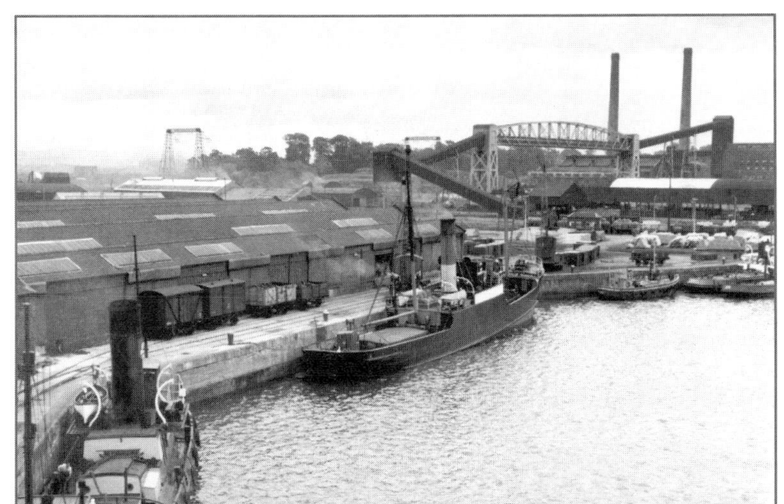

The Docks, West Side c1955 P113045

We can see two of the four tugs that the corporation, who ran the docks, had bought. Three were named after councillors who had supported the movement to build the docks: they were the 'Charles Hearn', the 'John Herbert' and the 'Frank Jamieson', and the fourth was the 'Hewitt'. The docks had an area of 850ft by 300ft, equalling forty acres of water. There was also a dock basin at the river entrance of four and half acres of water. In the fifties there was a weekly delivery of bananas from the Windward and Leeward Islands, and a ripening shed had to be built on the docks.

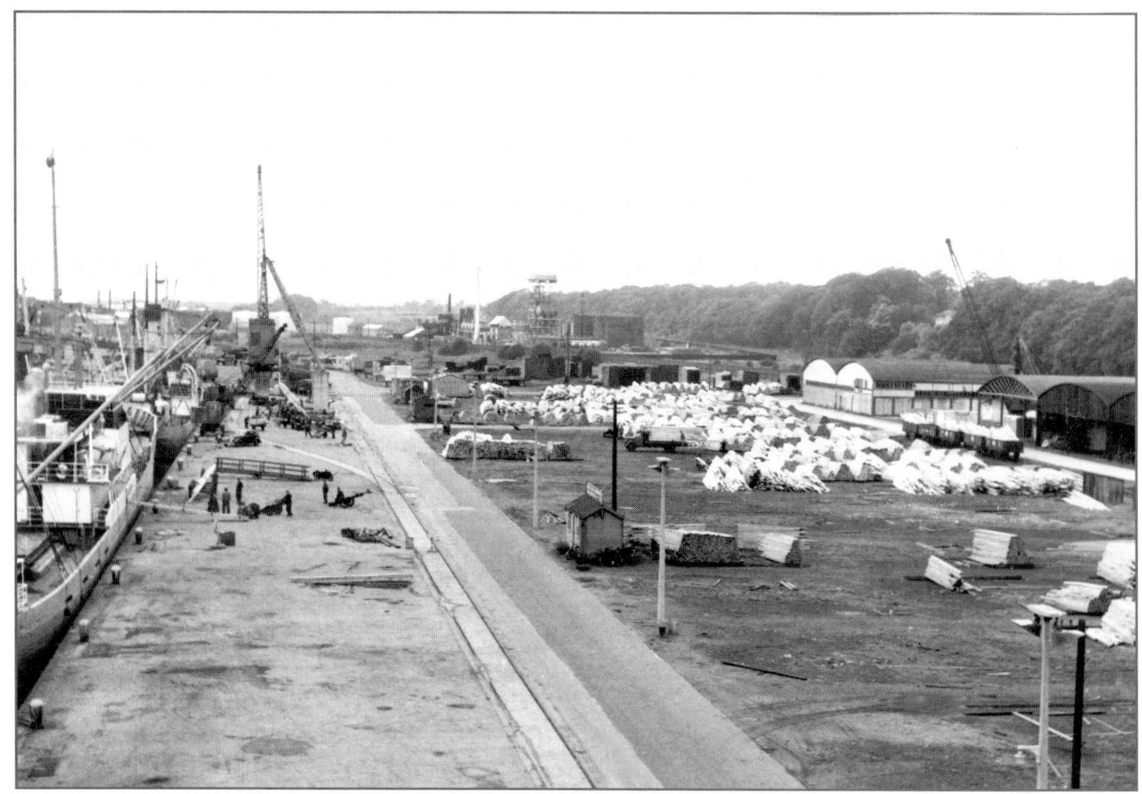

The Docks, North Side c1960 P113049

In this photograph we can see wood stacked for seasoning within the dock area. Frequent visitors here were the Russian ships bringing in hardwoods. In October 1964 the Russian MV 'Igarkales' caught fire while it was still half unloaded. Firefighting was hampered by the fact that the crew spoke no English, and could not be understood when they raised the alarm. Owing to the Cold War, the Russian captain was under orders not to let anyone British on board, which made matters even worse. Union troubles did not help the port, which in all honesty was never a great success - at best it broke even. In the 1960s weekly freight services to Ireland were launched, sailing to Londonderry, Portrush, Dublin and Waterford, and the port was amongst the first to offer a roll-on, roll-off service for taking vehicles over to Ireland.

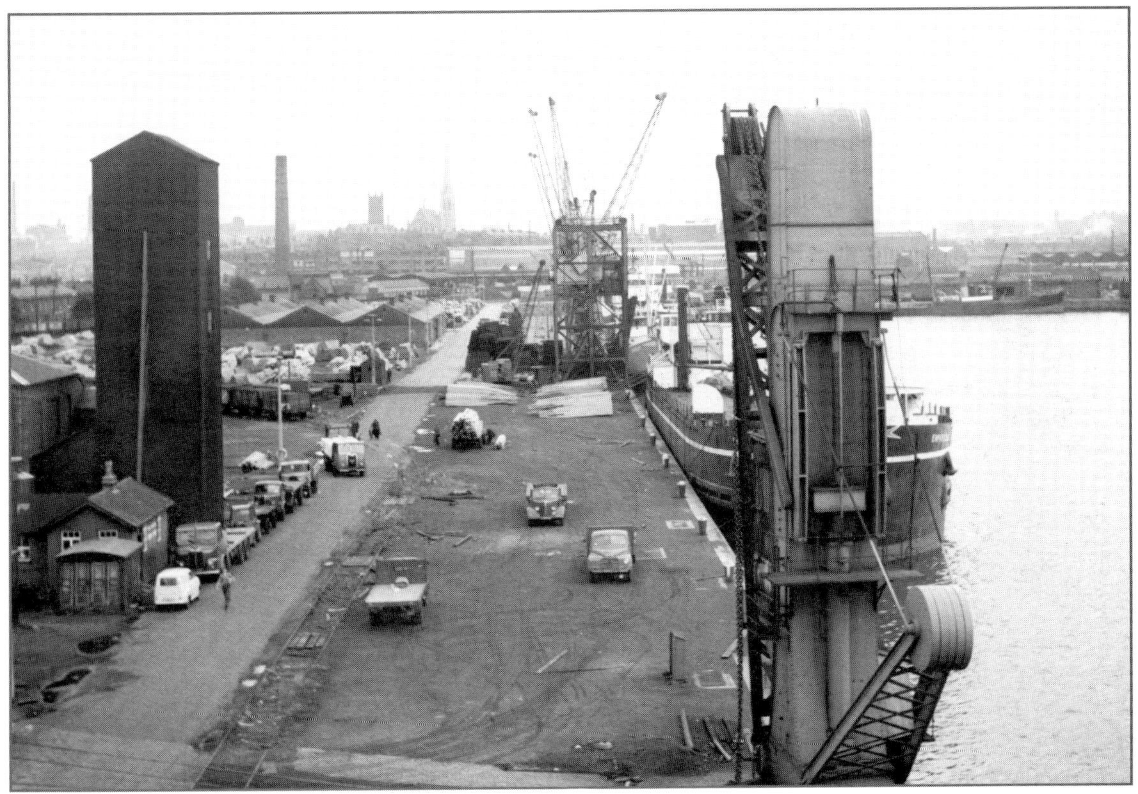

The Docks, North Side c1960 P113050

The fight to save the docks was a long and bitter battle. The council had been losing money for year on year, and felt that the drain on council rates was not good for the town. There were so many other uses for the money which was being used to prop up the ailing docks. Yet they did provide work for local people: at the time of our photograph around 500 worked there, and many more provided ancillary services. By October 1981 the council were deep in talks to re-develop the dock area. Today this area is offices and supermarkets, and the re-development is thought to be a success.

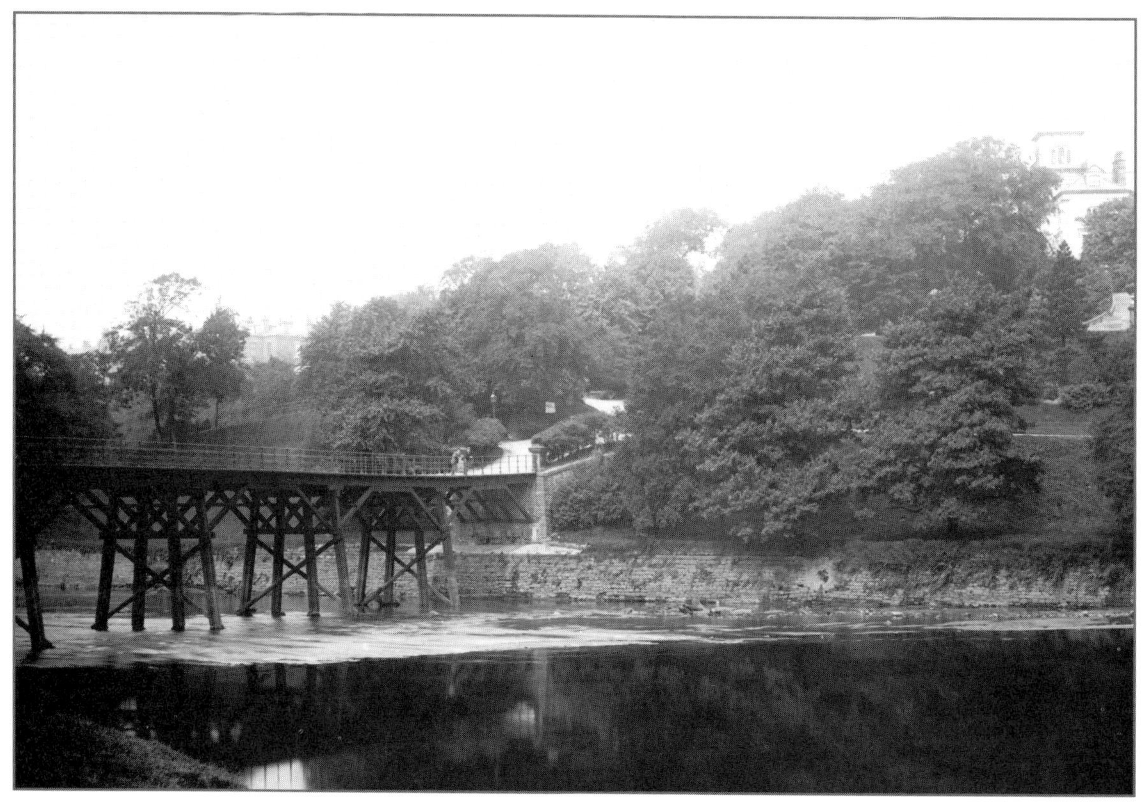

The Old Tram Bridge 1893 33100

Here we see a lovely tranquil picture of the Old Tram Bridge over the River Ribble; it was built to take a tram line over the river some time before 1829. The tram lines were removed in 1859, and for the last 140 years this has been a footbridge over the river. Today it is the only footbridge over the Ribble at Preston. A company was formed in the very early 1800s to build a canal from Chorley to Lancaster. It completed the section to Walton and the northern section from Preston to Lancaster, but money ran out before it could complete the aqueduct over the Ribble, which was the most costly part of the whole project. It was decided to join the two complete canal sections with a tramway. Goods were unloaded at Walton, and continued on horse-drawn waggons, and then on steam-drawn waggons up the incline to Avenham. After passing under Fishergate, the waggons were unloaded back on to the canal at Aqueduct Street to complete the journey. It sounds a makeshift arrangement, and it was never a satisfactory solution.

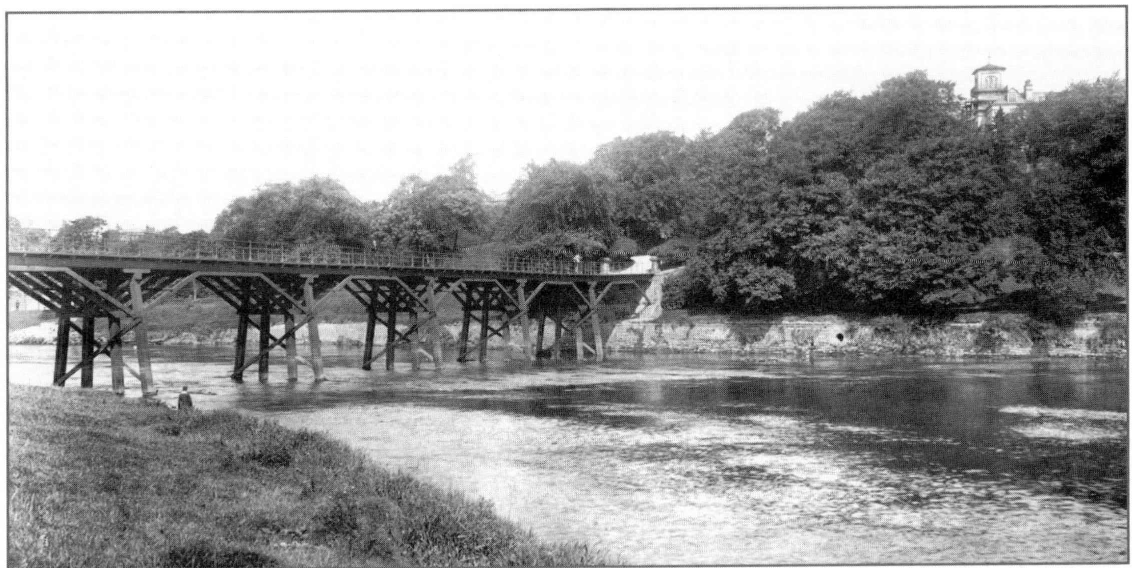

The Tram Bridge 1903 50073
Having Avenham Park in the background does enhance the pleasure of a walk over the bridge. Avenham Tower can be seen in the trees to the right, and the paths lead away to Frenchwood. The bridge was designed by William Cartwright, the canal's civil engineer, who was also an optician in Preston and an inventor of some note. In 1936 the swollen river flooded some allotments and washed away a hen shed, which hit the bridge. Without much debate the broken bridge was repaired, and the citizens continued to enjoy their promenades. Some early postcards refer to the Walk as 'Lovers' Lane'.

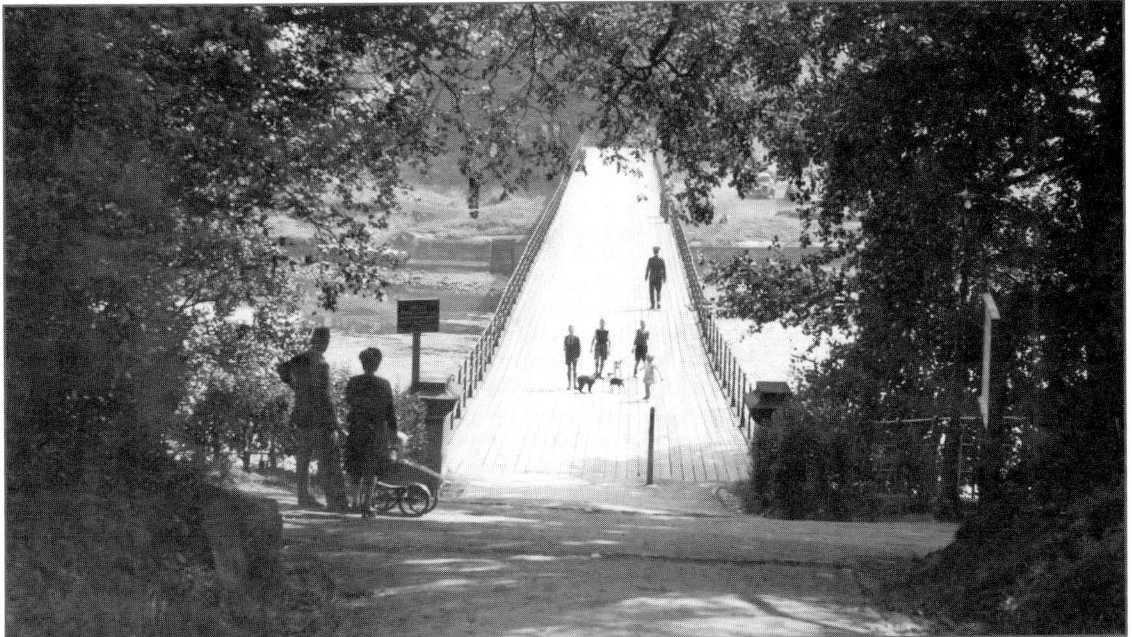

The Tram Bridge c1955 P113007
The bridge started to show its age soon after our photograph was taken, and by the mid 1960s it was declared unsafe. Again it could have been pulled down, but it was saved and rebuilt to the original design in concrete. It is now the only footbridge over the River Ribble here, and a great asset to the parks and recreation facilities of Preston.

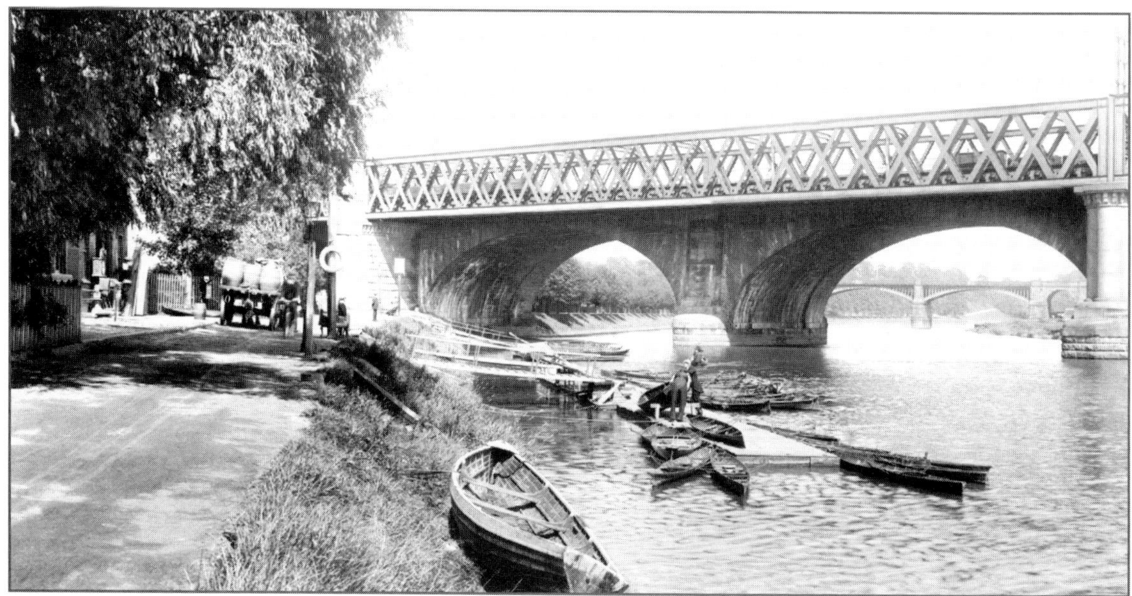

The River Ribble 1903 50077

Here we see the river bank of the Ribble just west of the main railway bridge at the end of South Meadows. The dray on the left is delivering to the Pleasure Boat Inn, which is hidden by trees on the left of the picture. The landlord hired out boats by the hour, as well as providing trips up and down the river. He had the unfortunate name of Mr Crook. The railway bridge here was built in 1838 by North Union Railways for the Preston to Wigan line at a cost of £70,000, and is now part of the west coast main line.

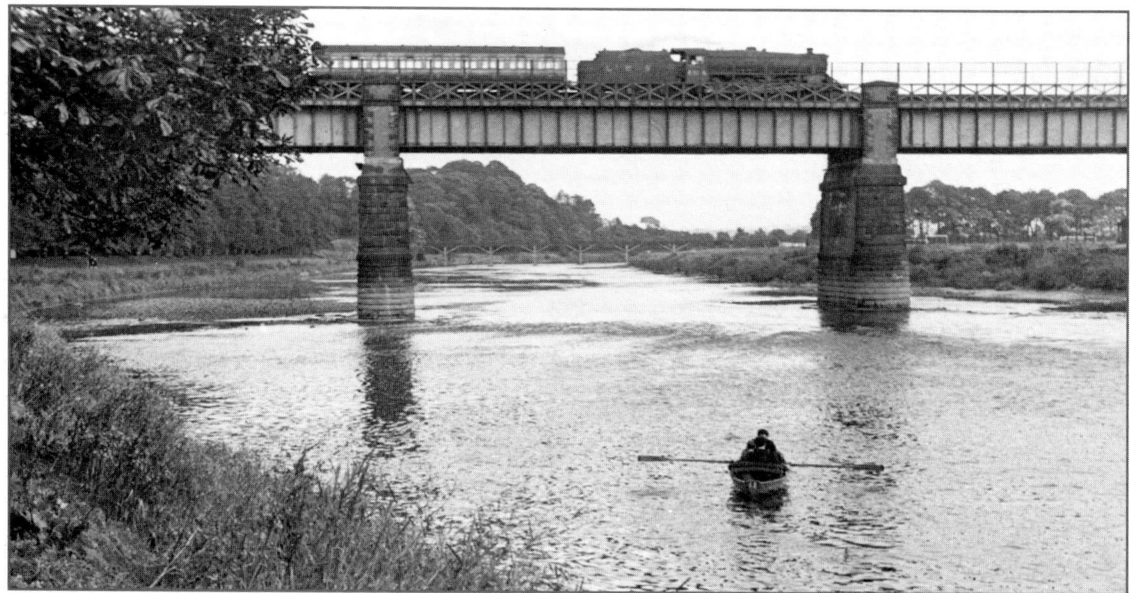

The River Ribble from Miller Park c1955 P113018

This wonderful nostalgic photograph shows steam engine 'black 5', the work-horse of the LMS region, heading south with non-corridor stock on a local, probably to Bamber Bridge and on to Blackburn. The three young lads out in a rowing boat sum up the simple pleasures of the mid 1950s, the quiet void before the rock 'n roll era and the Swinging 60s began. Today, it is quite hard to get down to the river in some places, but the Ribble is still there waiting to be reinvented.

The Fifties & Swinging Sixties

In 1945, as Preston emerged from the six years of war, it faced a future of immense change. This change was slow at first, owing to the lack of building materials and then to the on-off investment programmes of the late 1960s. It is a well-recorded fact that Preston had the first real piece of motorway in Britain: the Preston Bypass opened in 1959. I remember the glamour of the all-night restaurant in the service area where pop-groups would sit in dark glasses eating steak and chips at 2.00am just to be 'groovy'. One sad sign of the late 1950s all over Britain was the closure of cinemas, those wonderful palaces where teenagers did much of their courting and couples got to know each other between many a proposal (marriage proposal, that is). In 1955 the King's Palace Theatre closed, and 1957 saw the shutting down of the Royal Hippodrome, which had 2,500 seats. The Hippodrome was cleared to make way for a C & A Store on Fishergate, and live theatre looked to be going the way of the cinemas. Television had arrived, and life would never be the same again.

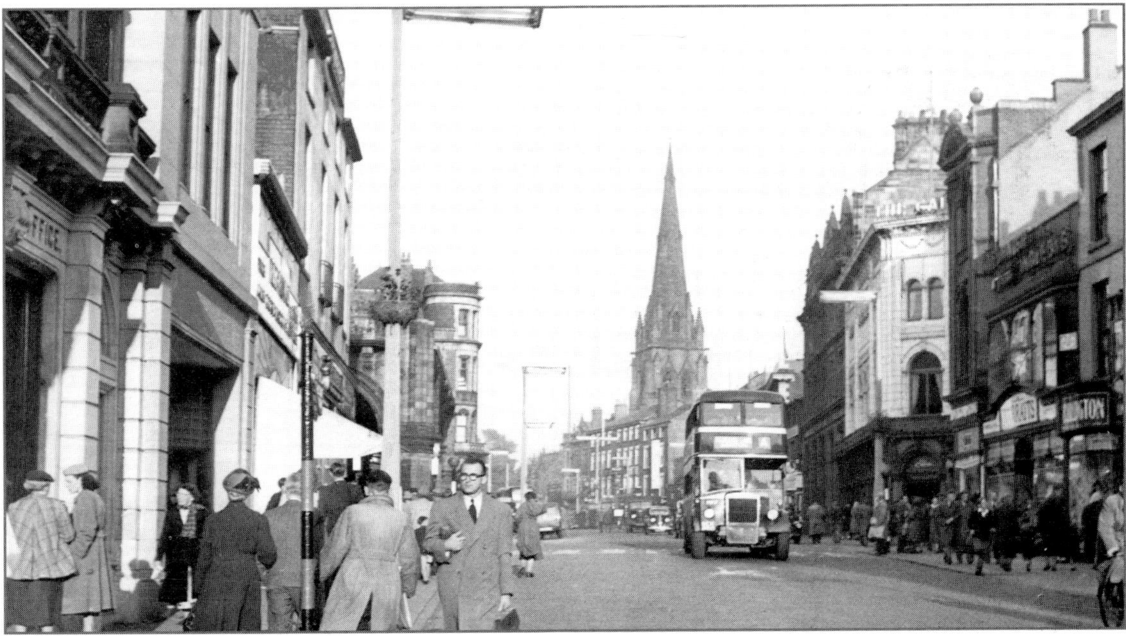

Fishergate c1955 P113026

Still the main street of Preston, Fishergate shows off some of its very varied shops. The spire of the parish church dominates the centre of the photograph. Corporation buses - how fondly they are remembered today! They were on time, they had a conductor to help and take fares, and the prices never seemed to change. On the left of the picture just behind the lamp post you can just make out the remains of Preston Town Hall, which had burnt down in 1947. These remains stayed there until October 1961, when a clearing-away programme began.

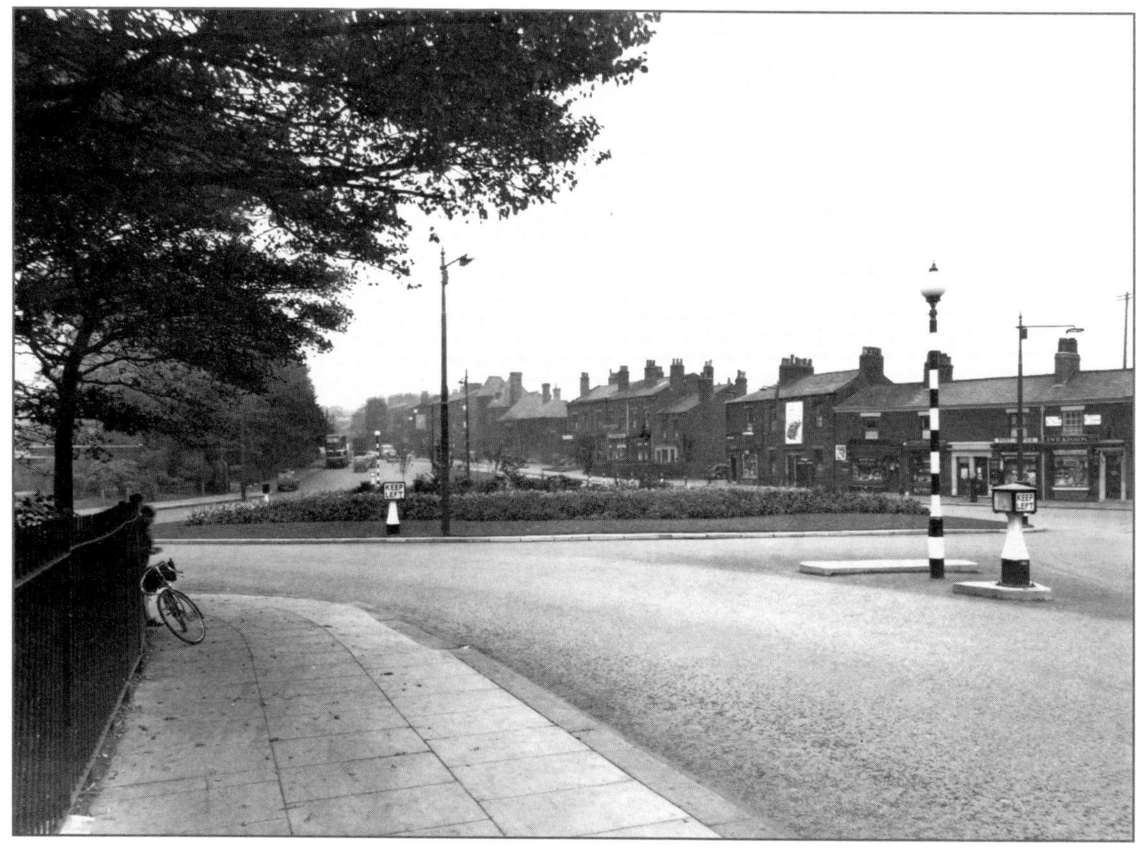

Fishergate Hill c1955 P113038
We are looking into town towards the railway station up Fishergate Hill. It really is a shame to say so, but to many people from the cities of Liverpool and Manchester and the South Lancashire towns Preston was just an obstacle, a marker on the journey to Blackpool. The town has always had a problem in dealing with traffic coming into the town, and with the traffic hell-bent on getting past Preston. It is a never ending problem, as the number of cars on the roads still increases. To the right is the road from Liverpool, Wigan, Warrington and Widnes. Our photographer was standing on the road that continued past the electrical engineering factory, past the docks and on to Blackpool. 'We're not opening any ale till we get to Preston' and 'I'll turn the lights off in the coach at Preston' have been said many times, as people travelled to and from Blackpool.

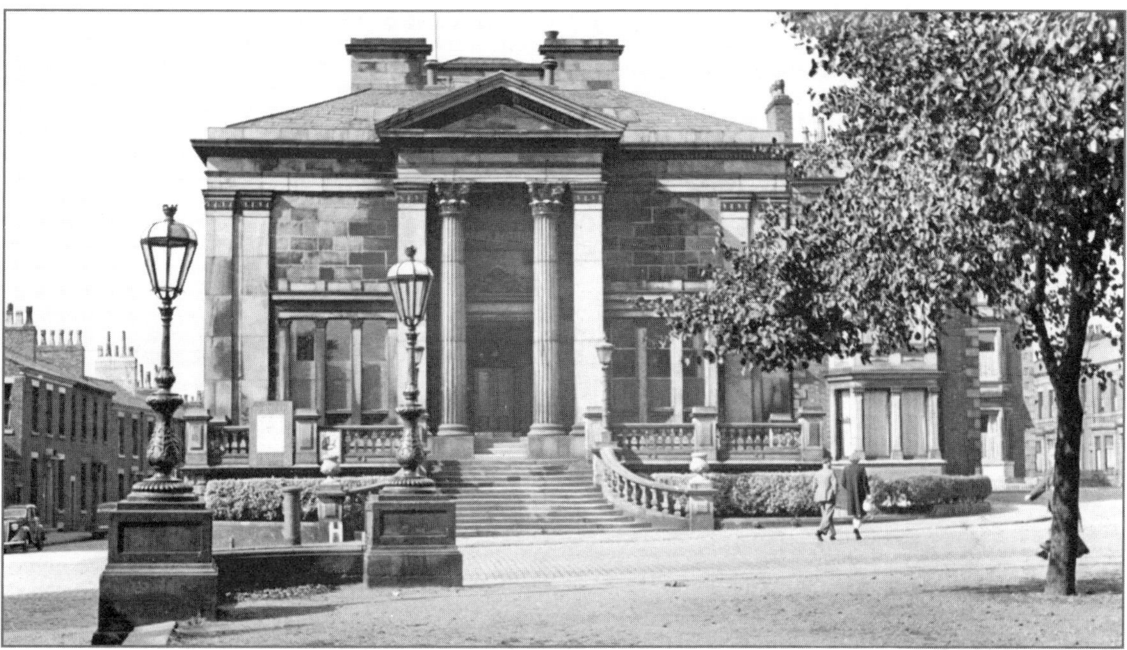

The Harris Institute c1955 P113017
The Institute for the Diffusion of Useful Knowledge has stood up well to the passing of time. At this point it is the Art College, and the rock-pop era is about to break in on our rather sedate photograph. The duffle-coats and beatniks, the anti-war protests and folk clubs that started then are just a year or so away, and now only a memory.

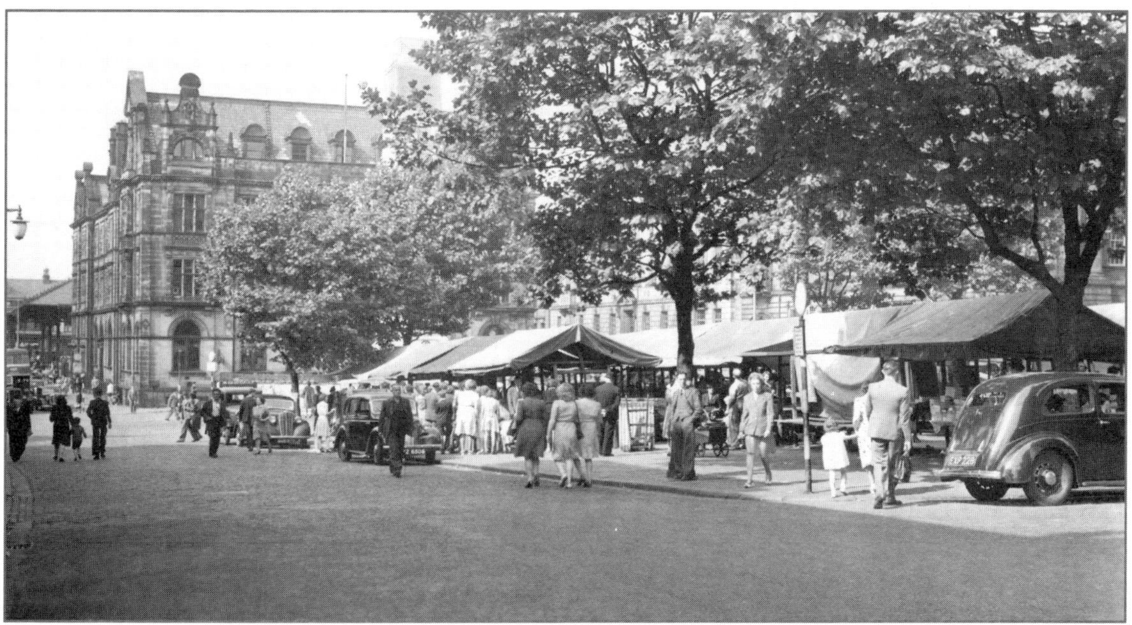

The Market Place c1955 P113015
Preston also had a covered market, so this busy scene could be the yearly Pot Market, which took place in the square for eight days every August. Traditionally it was a noisy fair, with the stall-holders allowed to shout to advertise their wares. Two centuries ago, Preston had a market every Saturday at first light, then a linen market, and then when everything was sold, a fish market and a cattle market.

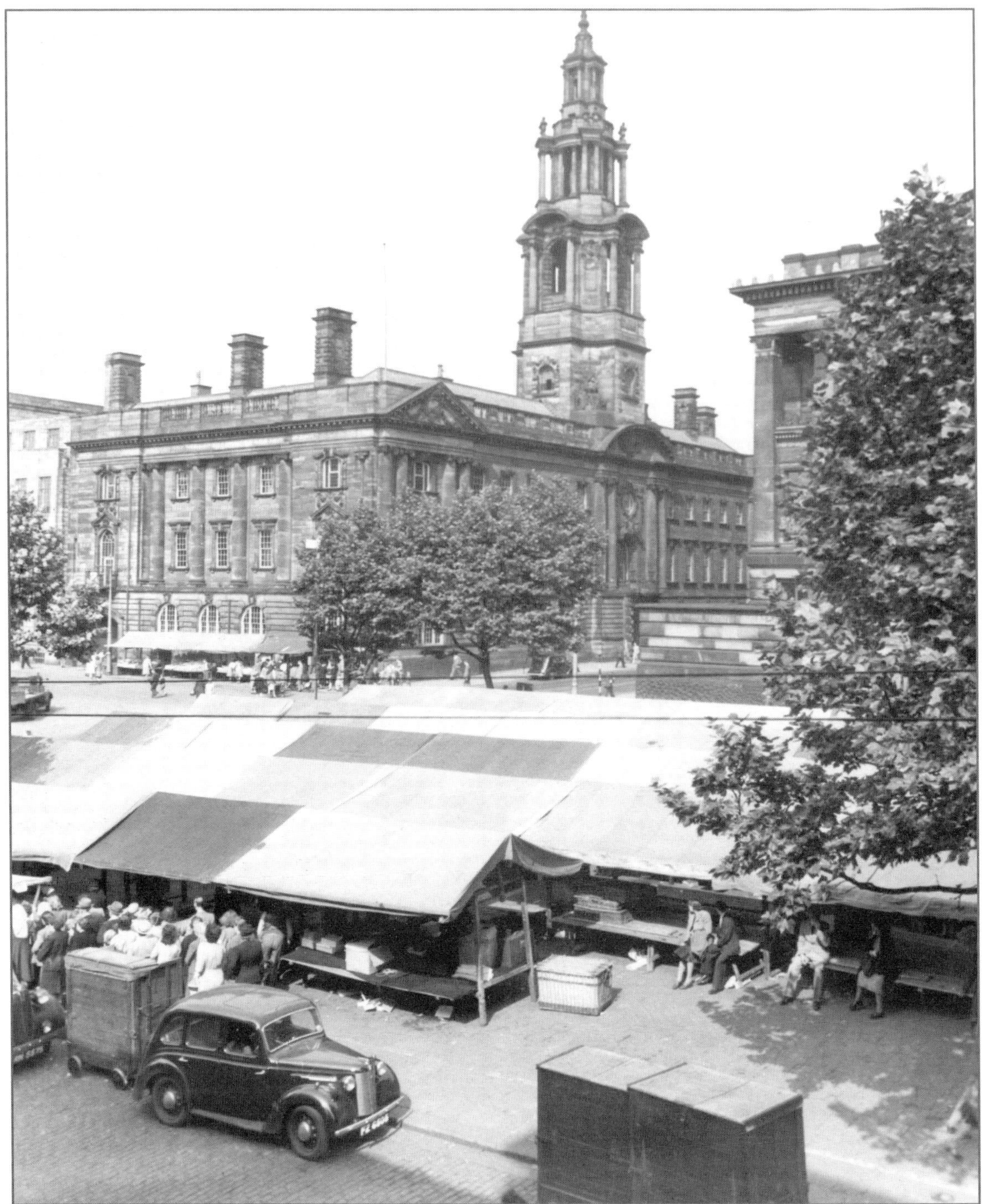

The Market Square c1955 P113014
This view shows the August Pot Market. Locals refer to this area as the 'Flag Market'. On the left of the picture you can see some of the locals listening to the patter of an auctioneer telling them of all the wonderful bargains he was about to let them have. The squarish carts were used to carry the pottery to and from the markets. A local delicacy sold from stalls around the market was black-eyed peas with vinegar or mint sauce, and new potatoes dripping in best butter with mint sauce. Lovely!

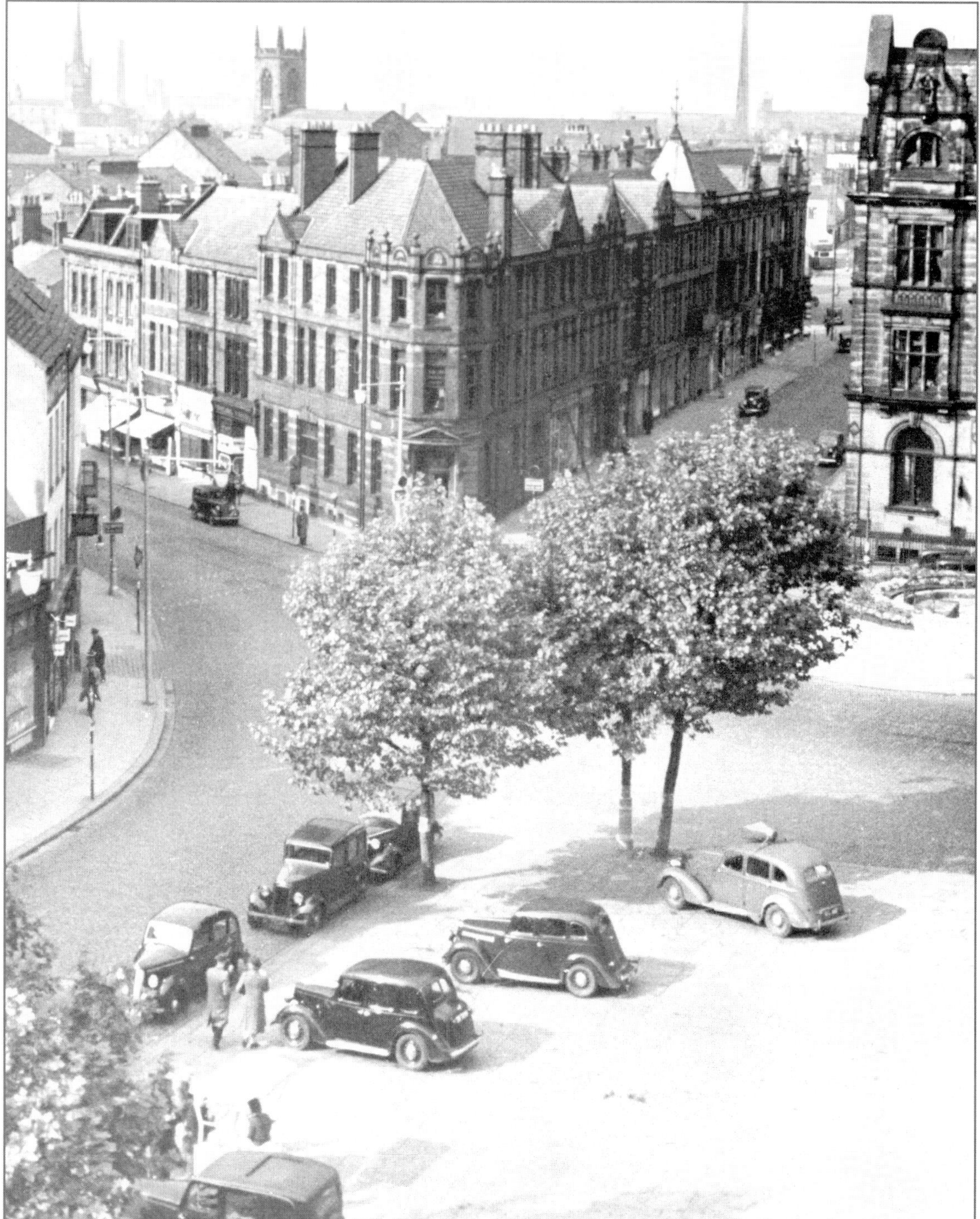

Friargate c1955 P113022

An unusual view that can only have been taken from the remains of Preston Town Hall. The Flag Market area lies below our photographer, and Cheapside runs at the bottom left-hand corner. Friargate is the street running off to the left, and Market Street runs alongside the Post Office, which is just caught on the right of the picture. Parking in Market Square is a luxury which we have not been allowed for many years now.

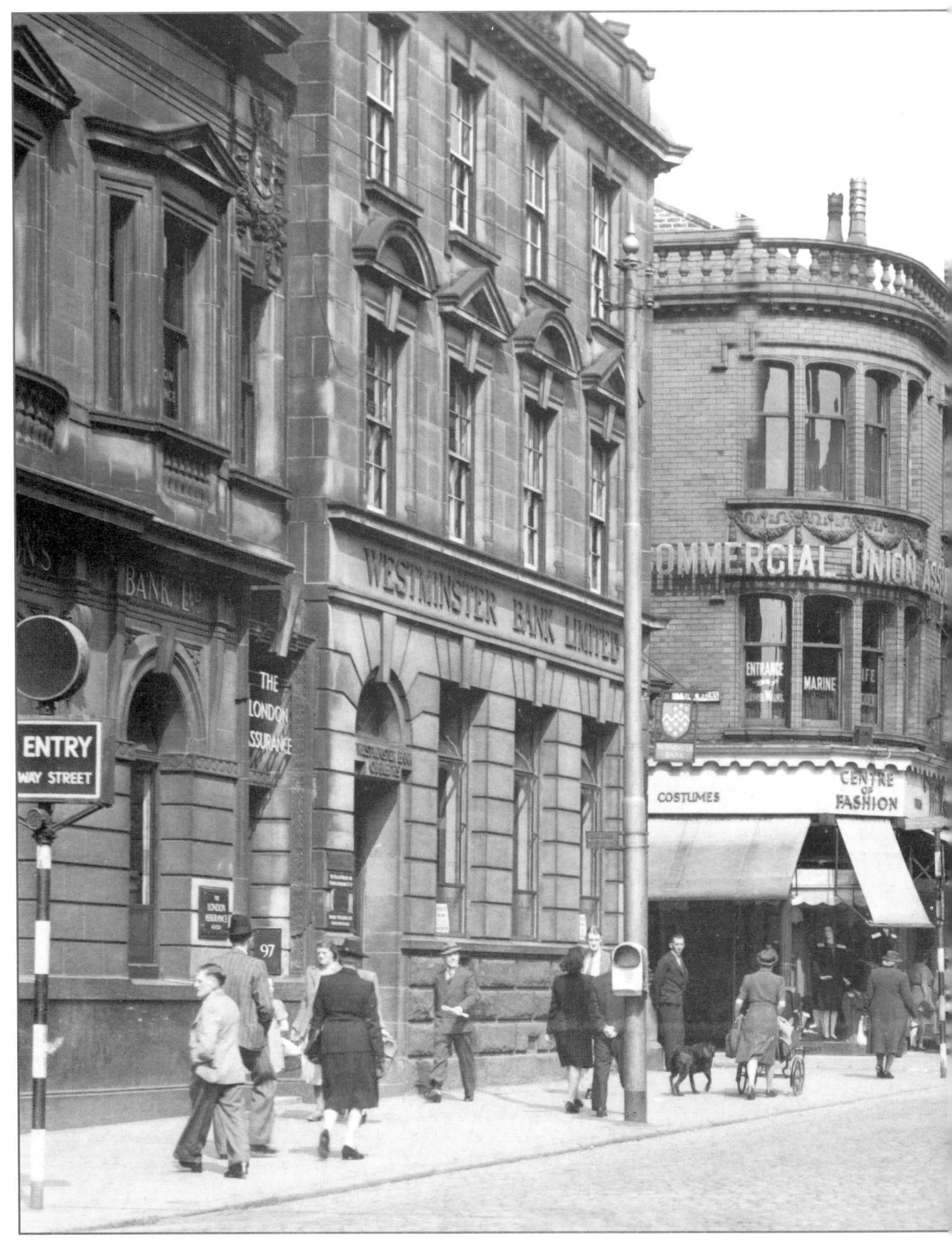
ENTRY
WAY STREET
BANK Ld
THE
LONDON
WESTMINSTER BANK LIMITED
97
ENTRANCE
MARINE
COSTUMES
CENTRE OF FASHION

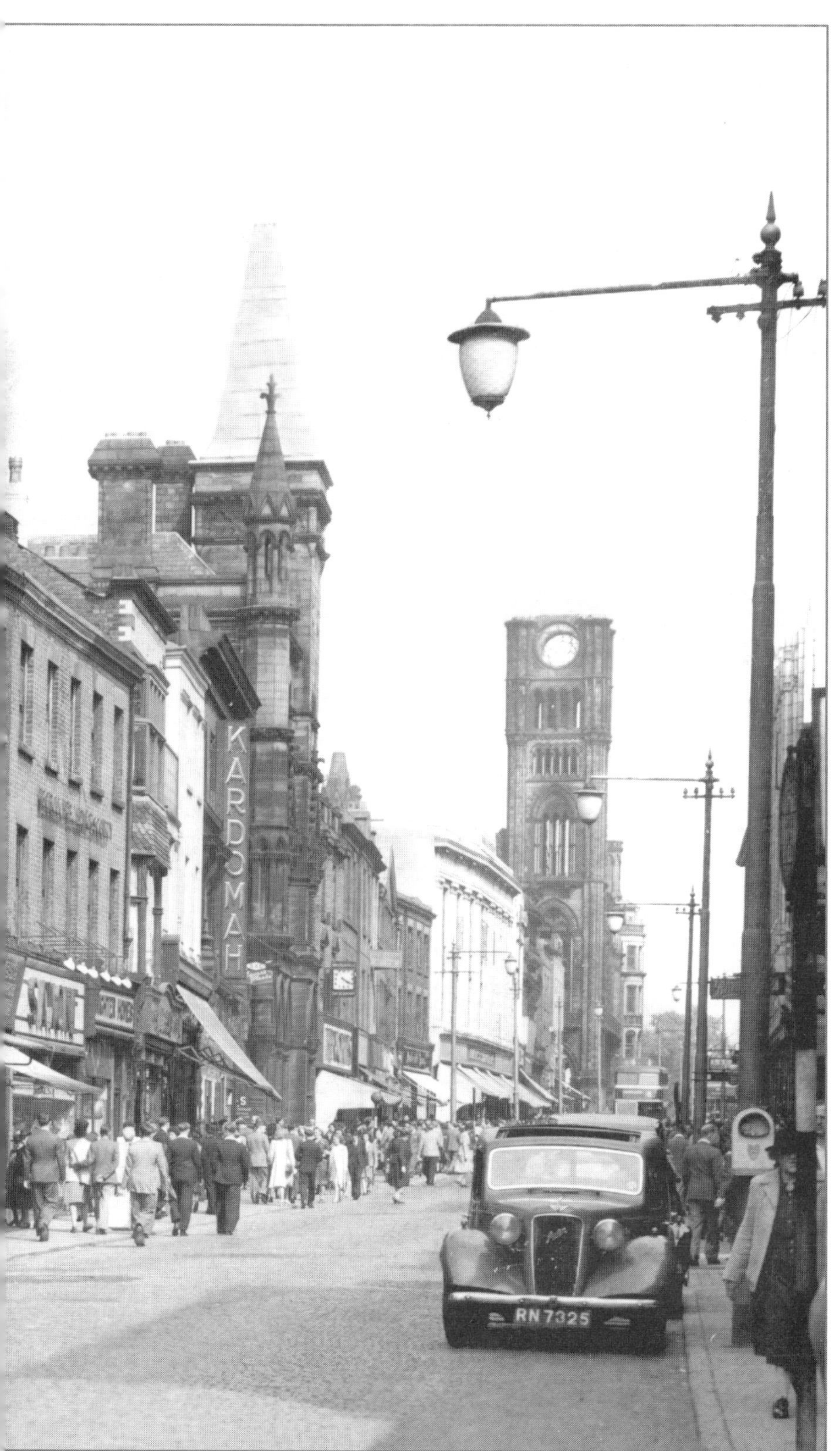

Fishergate c1955

P113009

This view was taken from around the Corporation Street corner. We can see the one-way sign on the street, so the area was having traffic problems nearly half a century ago. Two banks and two insurance companies occupy the left of the picture, and there is a Kardomah Cafe just further up next to Fishergate Baptist Church. It was this area that was badly damaged in 1991 when the IRA blew up the RAF and Navy Recruitment Office in Fishergate. Fortunately, there was no loss of life, and though the church lost many of its windows, it was restored.

Friargate and the War Memorial c1960 P113076A

Friargate was still full of traffic at this time, and not the pedestrianised area it is today. The friary that gave its name to the street was founded in the early 13th century by the Franciscan order of Grey Friars; they also founded the Leper Hospital of St Mary Magdalen, and Magdalen Land became Maud Land.

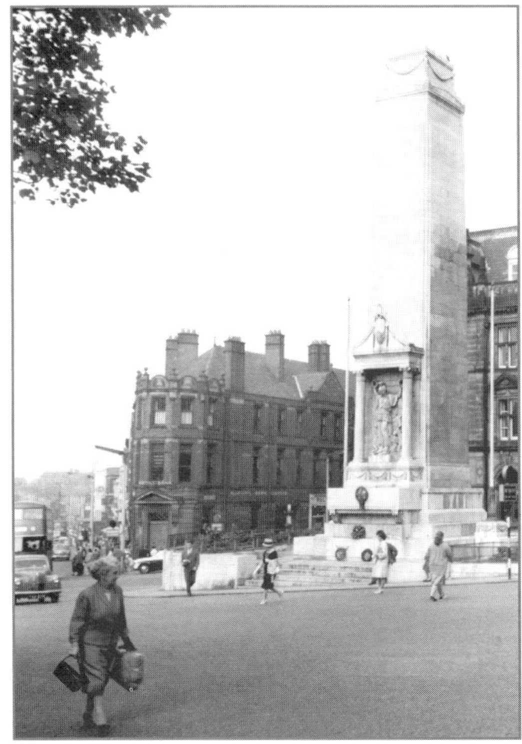

The Approaches to the Covered Market c1960 P113076B

The Main General Post Office is on the left of the photograph. Gone are the days when it opened seven days a week from 7.30am to late in the evening. At the time of this photograph, the Post Office had announced the Saturday afternoon closing of the smaller offices and the cut-back of Sunday services in an effort to make more profit.

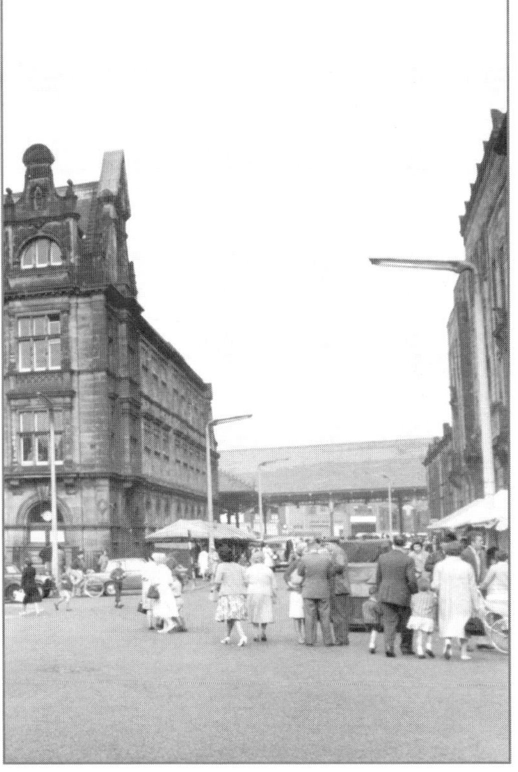

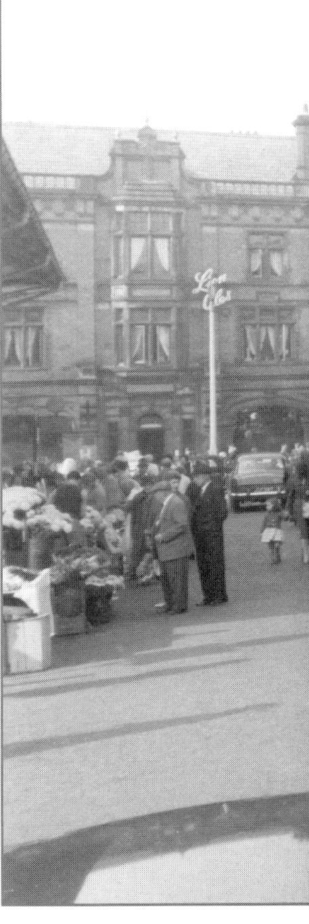

The Market c1960 P113(

This market was locally called the Covered Market. Plans were put in hand as early as 1868 to build a Market Hall on this site, which was previously know as the Orchard. On 6 Augu 1870 the roof of the mark fell in while it was being constructed, and after an enquiry the work was passed to a local shipbuild William Allsup. He decided not to put sides on the structure, and it was completed and finally opened in 1875. A new wholesale fruit and vegetab market opened in 1967.

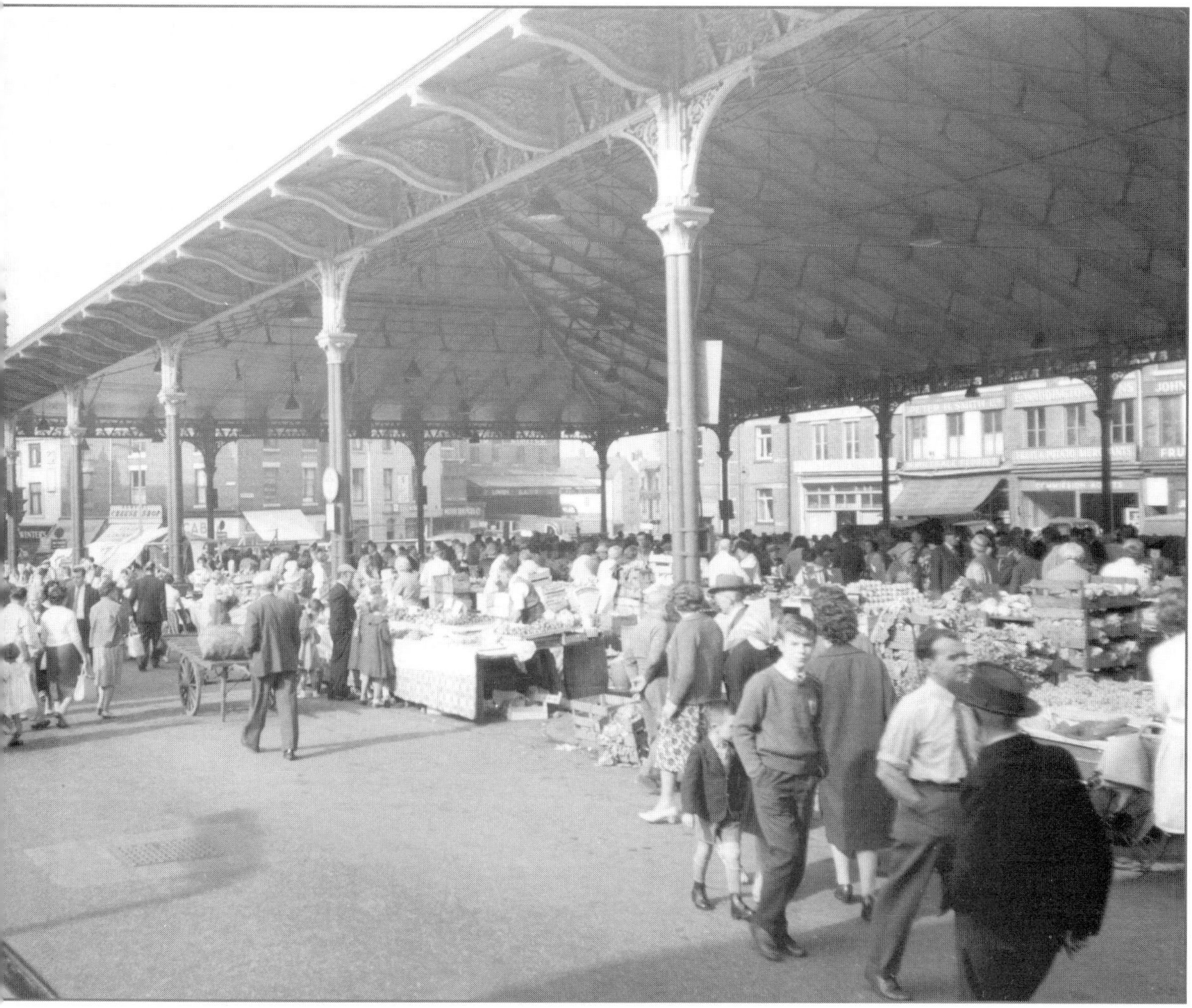

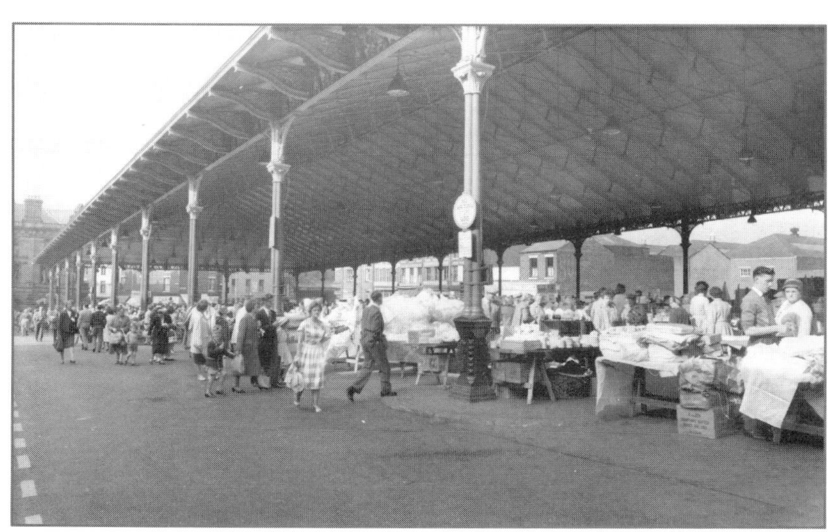

◄ **The Market c1960** P113075
There are bargains galore in the Covered Market. Our photograph does demonstrate just how open you were to the wind and rain, especially on the outside parts of the market. A hundred years earlier than our photograph, there would have been four cattle markets every week. Store cattle were sold on Monday, fat stock on Tuesday, store pigs on Wednesday and on Friday it was dairy cattle. Many of the animals were brought down the Lancashire Canal and held at the loading dock in the Marsh Lane/Corporation Street area.

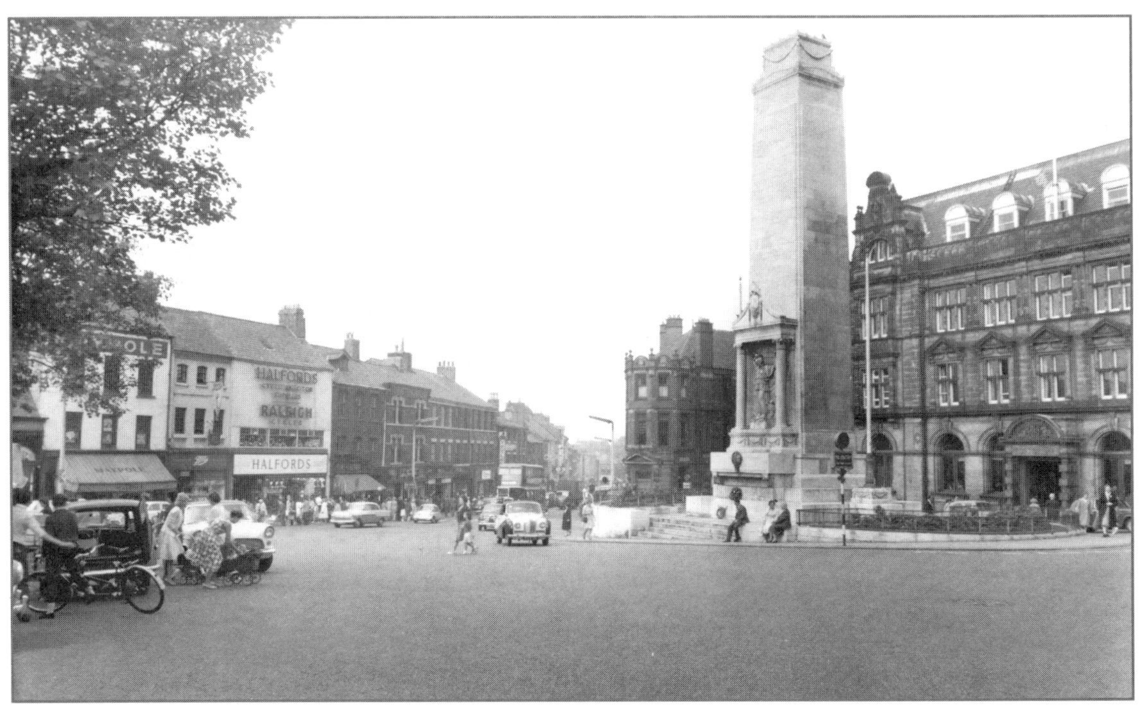

The Post Office and the Memorial c1965 P113077

This view looks from Market Square down Friargate. The Maypole Grocery Store (dried peas 1s 6d), Boots the Chemist and Halfords (everything for your Raleigh bicycle) are the shops overlooking the War Memorial, which by then had had the names added of the fallen of the Second World War.

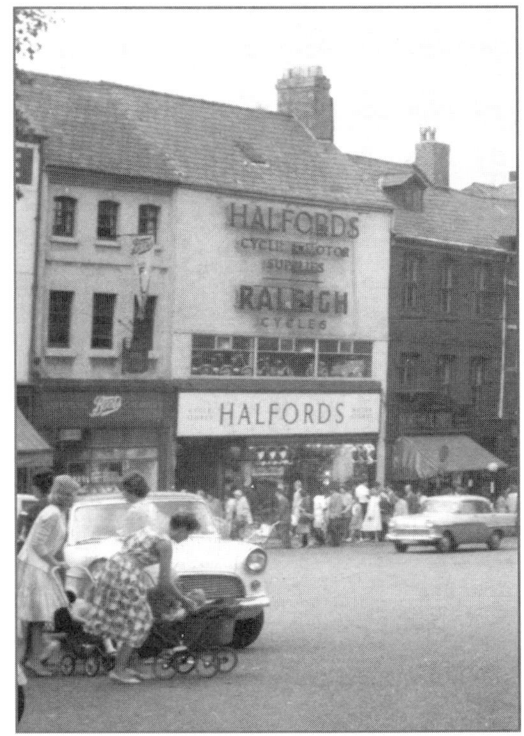

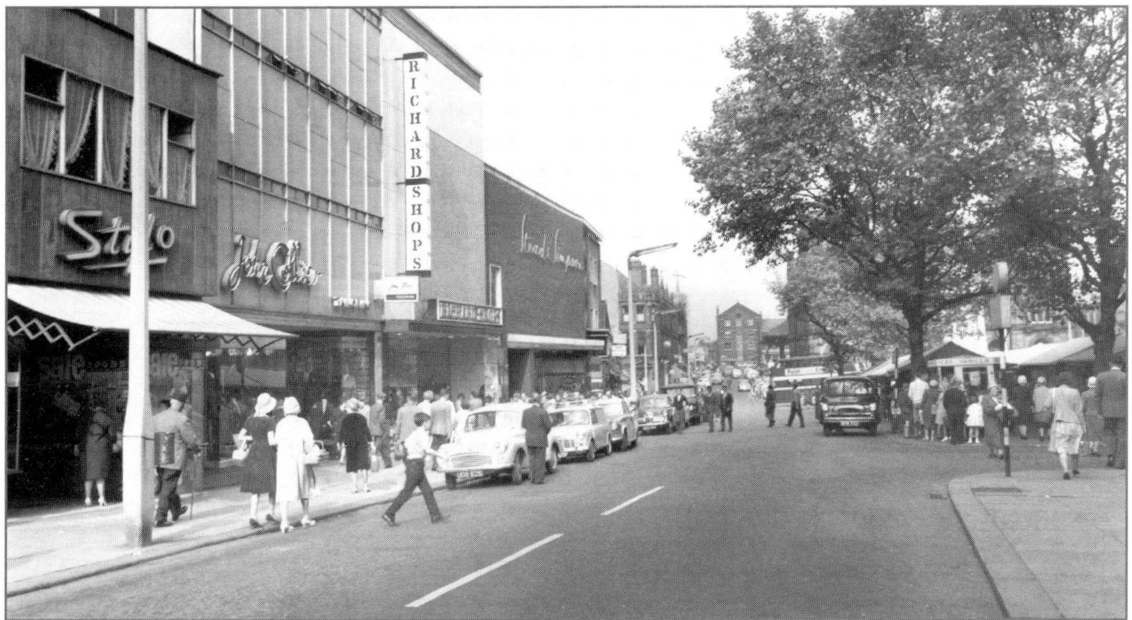

Cheapside c1960 P113079

Here we have a good view of the area that is to the west of Market Square. Stylo Shoe Shop, John Collier ('the window to watch'), Richard Shops and Stead & Simpson are among the many varied shops facing the Market. It is nostalgic to see the cars parked in the street - the Morris Minor and mini-vans for example - and no yellow lines and no parking meters. Those were halcyon days.

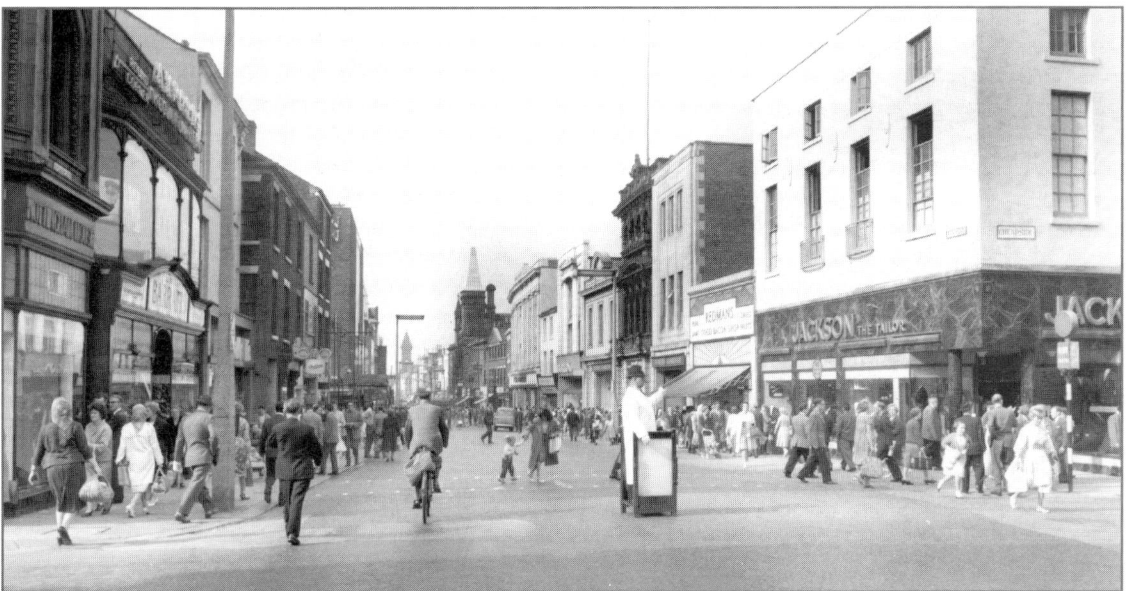

Fishergate c1965 P113080

Here is a picture taken from the point where Fishergate becomes Church Street. We are looking down towards the railway station in the distance; on the right is Cheapside, and Glover's Court is to the left. There are no traffic lights at this busy junction, so a policeman on his wood and canvas podium directs the traffic. Again we get a good idea of the diversity of shops in Preston, including Jackson's the Tailors, Redmans, 'the Good Bacon Shop', and many more that pulled in the shoppers from miles around the town.

The Parks of Preston

In the early Victorian years, a movement started to set aside green open spaces in our towns and cities where citizens could get a breath of fresh air, relax and take a stroll. Because Preston had the River Ribble, which lent a hand in giving the town an air of peacefulness, there was no rush to provide these sorts of facilities. It had Avenham Walk for the gentry -it had been there for over two hundred years already. In 1830 the town councillors started planning something for the people, a place to meet and play, a 'lung' for the hard-working town. Preston, and indeed the whole of Lancashire, was badly hit by the cotton famine caused by the American Civil War. Rather than spend money on unemployment pay, most Lancashire corporations took to the idea of creating work for at least some of the unemployed to keep them from starving; they used their labour to create these parks and public open spaces.

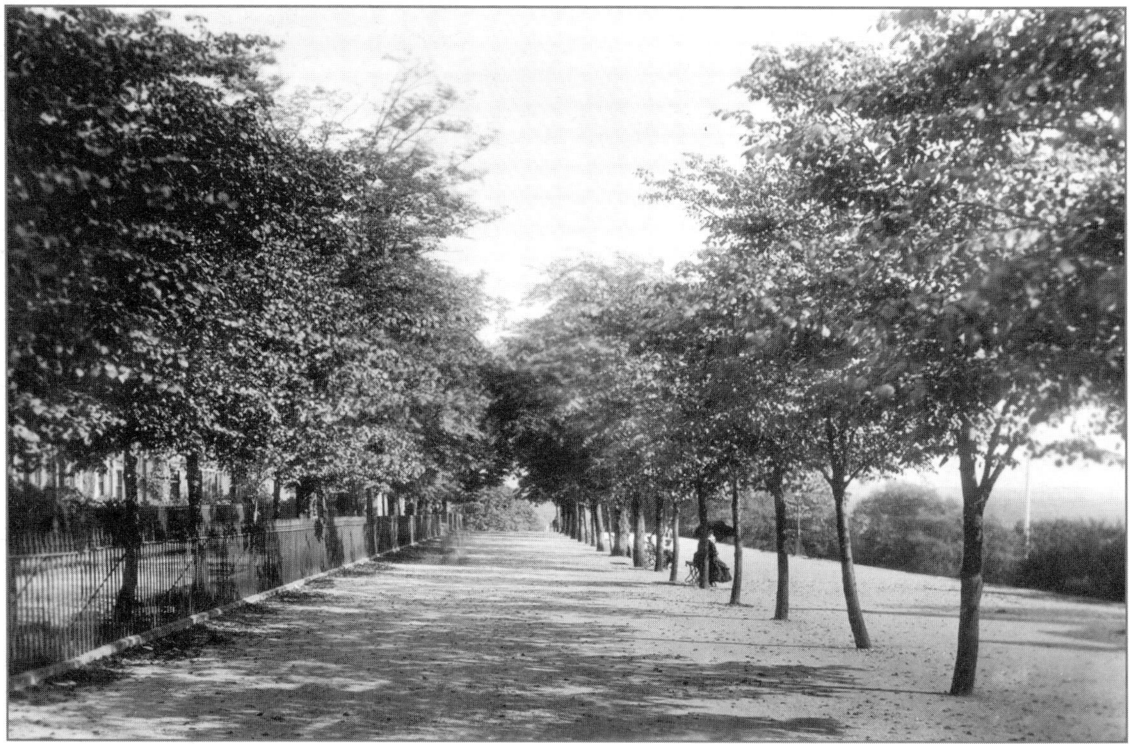

The Avenham Colonnade 1893 33090
With its double row of lime trees and its scenic views over the River Ribble, Avenham Walk has always been popular. It was marked out officially as early as 1728, though it is thought that it had been in use from 1696. Lime trees were chosen because they grow slowly; some of those in this picture are still there today.

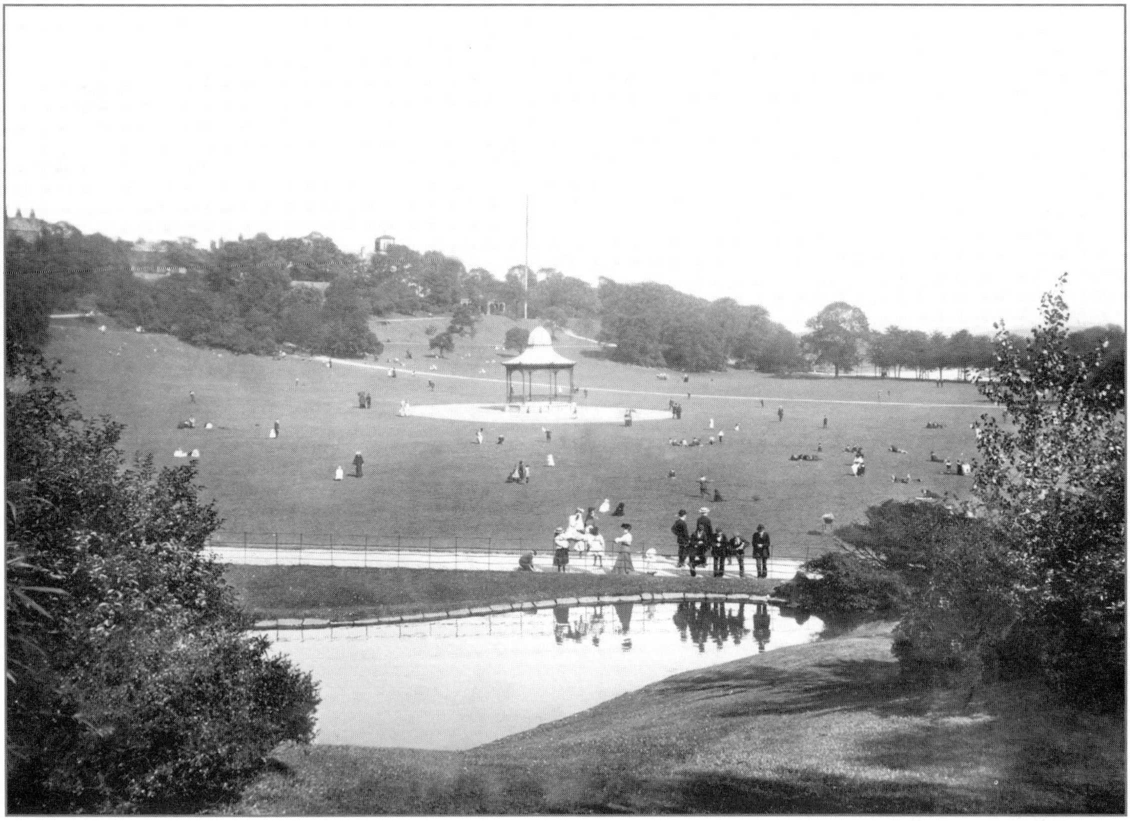

Avenham Park 1903 50087
This photograph, showing the pond, looks over what was known as the Valley. Both Avenham and Miller Park were started around 1864. As well as being lovely parks for the people, they were begun to provide work for some of the thousands laid off due to the cotton famine, which was caused by the American Civil War. The two parks are divided by a railway embankment that was already there.

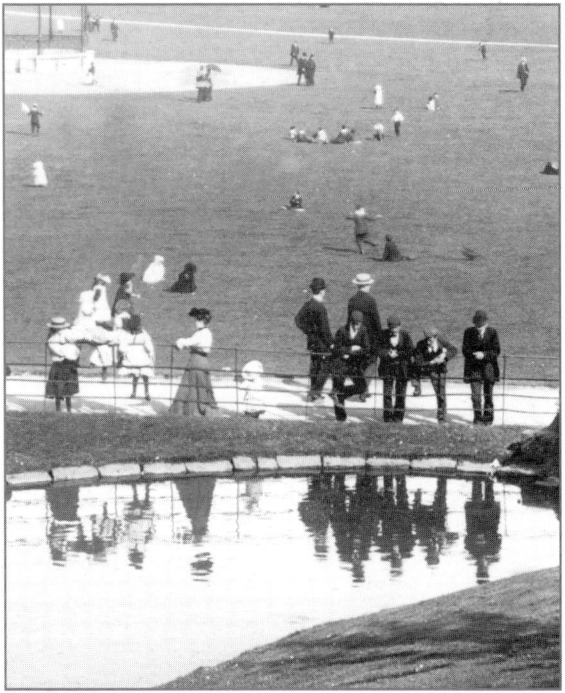

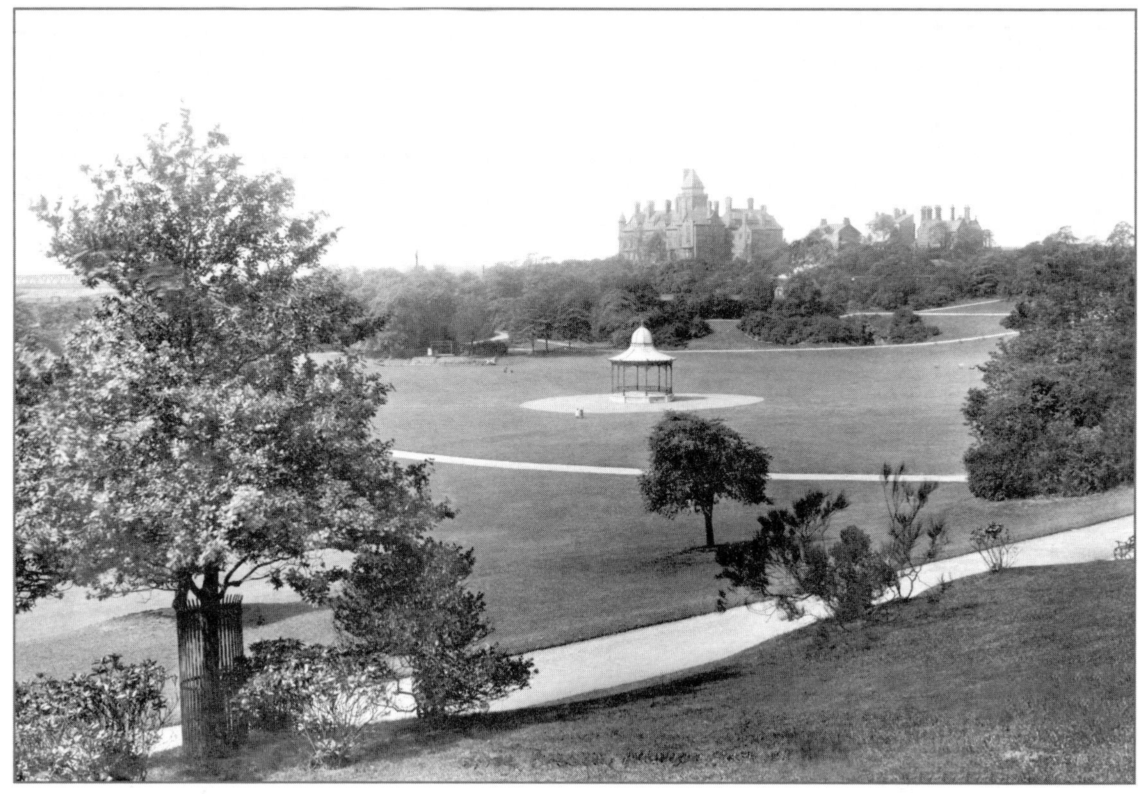

Avenham Park 1903 50072

This view of Avenham Park shows what a superb amphitheatre the area made. The Bandstand cost £450 when it was new in 1865; it lasted until it was dismantled in the late 1950s. The Park Hotel can be seen dominating the skyline, and the rolling hillocks in the park were ideal for Pace Egging, which had gone on almost since the park first opened. Pace Egging began because eggs were forbidden food during Lent, so any produced would be hard-boiled and kept until Good Friday. People then sent the eggs to church to be blessed, marking them in some way so that they knew their own eggs. All this has developed into the egg-rolling and games that still goes on today in Avenham Park on Easter Sunday and Monday.

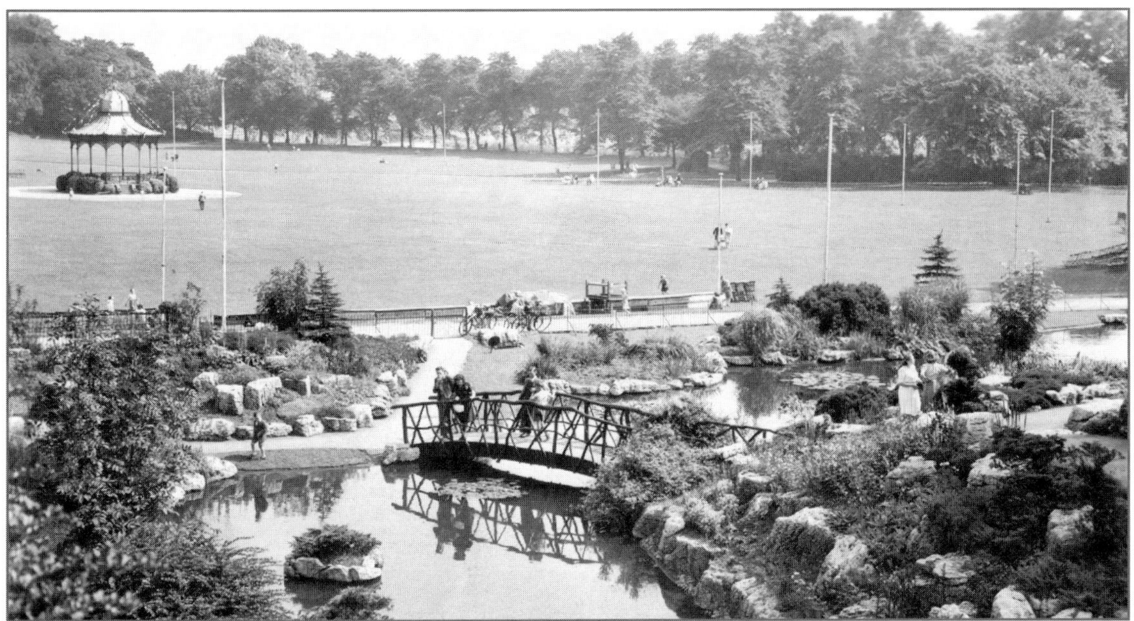

The Rock Gardens and Lawns, Avenham Park c1955 P113011

The Rock Gardens and Lawns Avenham Park c1955

The land for the park was given by Lt Col Cross, who lived in a large and impressive house at the Red Scar. The council bought the strip of land alongside the railway, and the area was ready to be developed. Before the Second World War, if the weather was very cold, the Fire Department would flood to a couple of inches the area between the Rockery and the Bandstand that you can see in this photograph, and people would come and ice-skate there.

The Park the Forty Steps 1924

A lot of thought and detail went into the planning of Avenham and Miller Parks, and there were some very interesting features built into both of them. The Avenham Tower and the Belvedere were two of the buildings in these Parks. Here we see the Forty Steps, with youngsters resting on them discussing the topics of their day.

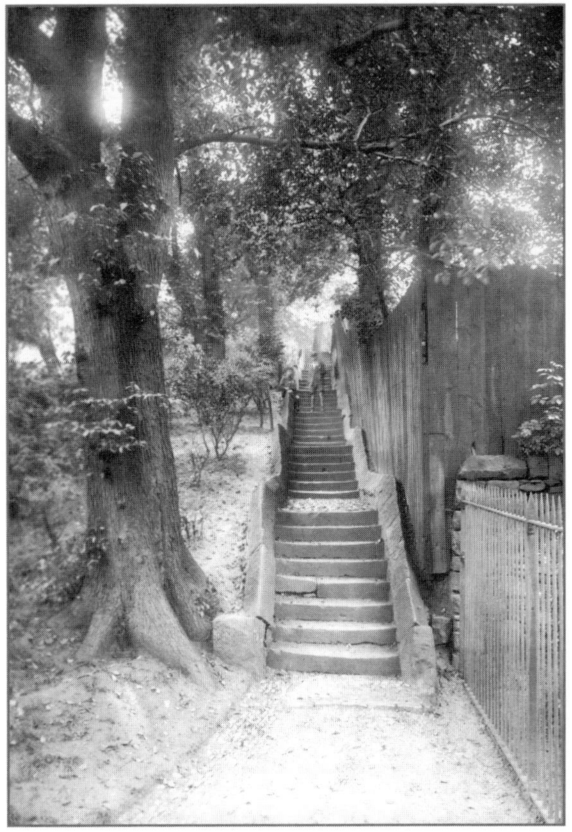

The Park, the Forty Steps 1924 75842

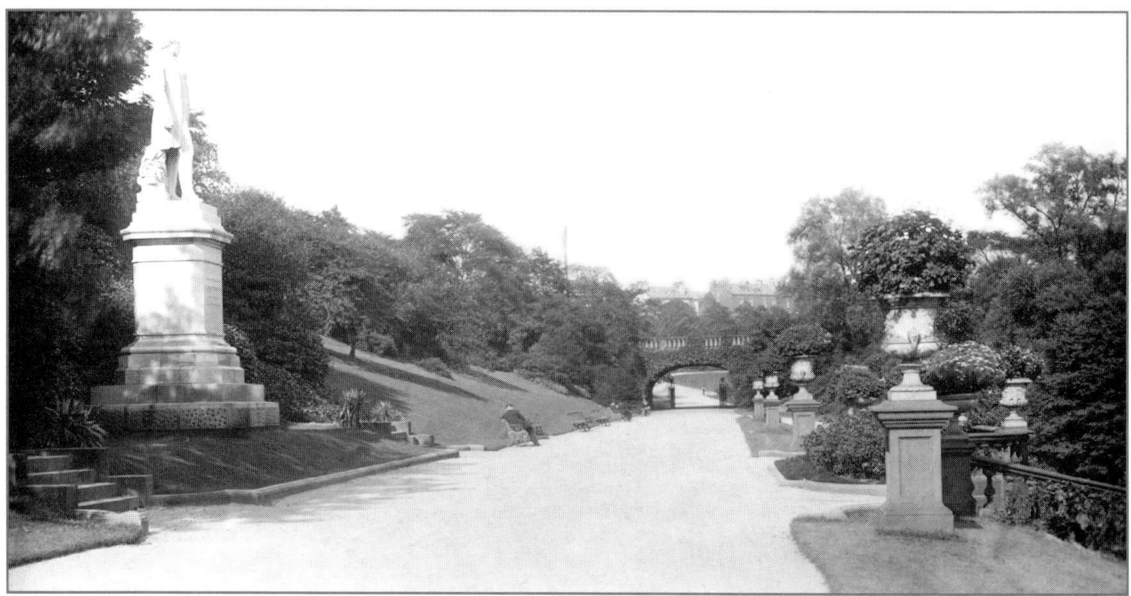

Miller Park 1893 33093
This is a view of the Derby Terrace. Avenham Park is on the other side of the railway bridge that can be seen in the centre, which was known as Ivy Bridge. When the Park opened, this area was known as the Broad Walk, but once the statue of the 14th Earl of Derby was placed here, it became known as Derby Terrace. Miller Park is the smaller of the two parks; it was laid out on eleven acres of land given by Alderman Thomas Miller in 1864. He died shortly after his bequest, and never saw his gift transformed into this beautiful park.

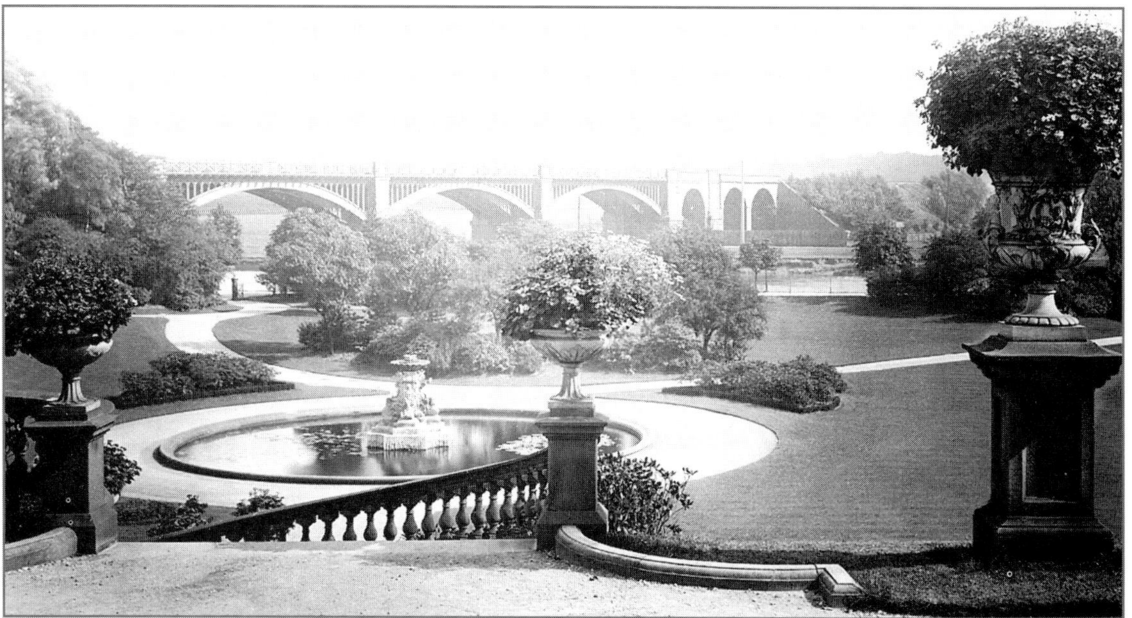

Miller Park 1893 33092
This is a view that Edward Geoffrey Stanley's statue enjoyed from the Derby Terrace. The bridge is the railway bridge over the River Ribble, and we can see the far bank clearly. Nearer to the camera is the fountain with four figures round the base that represent Earth, Air, Water and Fire, and we can see some of the classic urns which graced the steps and surrounds.

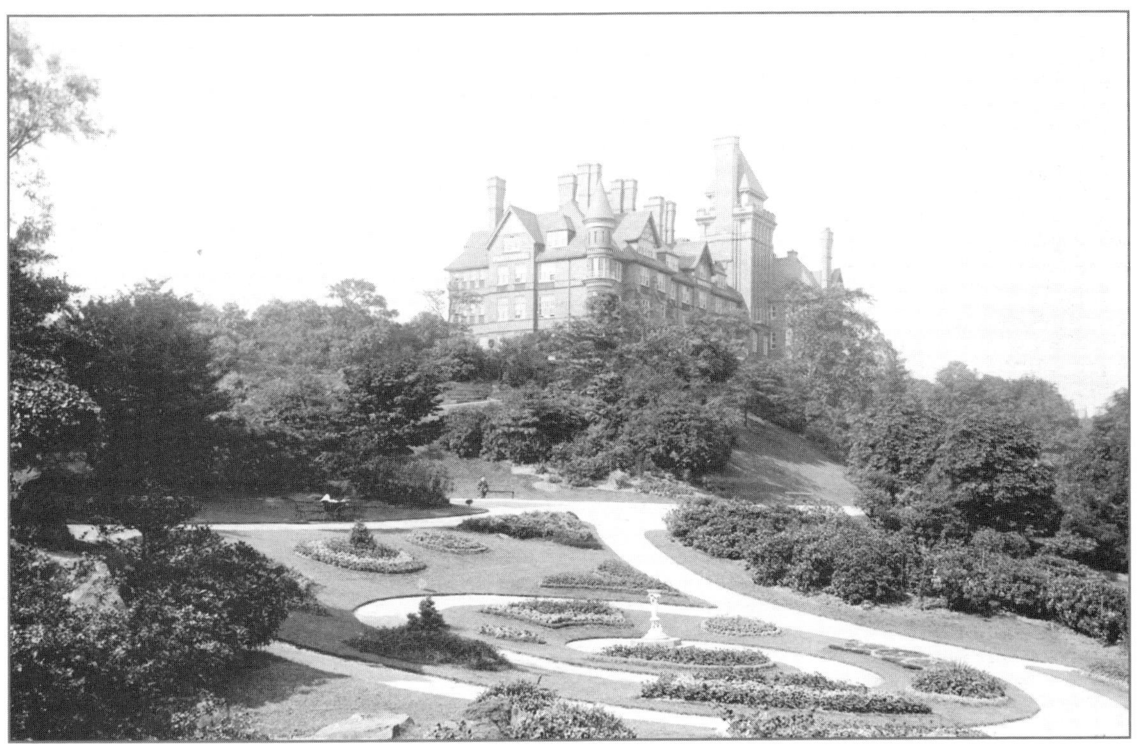

The Park Hotel 1893 33094

The Park Hotel stood on East Cliff. When the railway opened from London to Glasgow, it was considered 'detrimental to health to travel the full distance in one journey'. This hotel was built so that travellers could take an overnight break and continue refreshed the next day. There was a covered walk from the south end of the station to the hotel. It was designed by the Oldham architect Arnold Mitchell for the London & North Western Railway - he also designed the Winter Gardens in Blackpool. It cost £46,000 to build the hotel in red Ruabon brick and terracotta - these materials drew many comments, including 'gaudy'. The Park Hotel had four private suites, and only ten bathrooms to share between the fifty-five bedrooms.

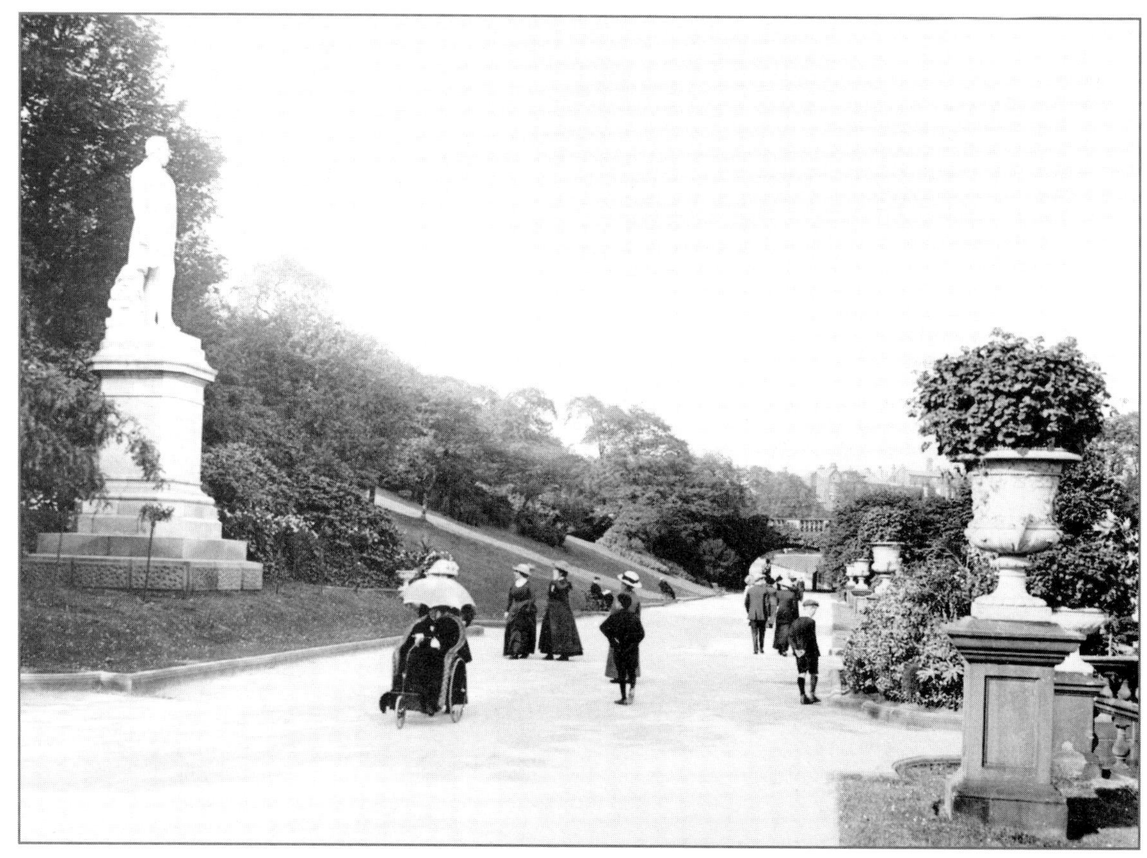

Miller Park 1913 65597
This view shows the Derby Terrace and its visitors. The Earl's statue was placed here after he donated over £5,000 to the Relief Fund to help the starving of Lancashire during the 1860s cotton famine. He had at one time been MP for Preston, but was MP for North Lancashire at the time. The pedestal is 15ft high and made of Aberdeen granite, and the statue is 11ft high and carved from Sicilian marble. The cost was £2,500, and £349 of that was raised by a penny subscription by workmen. In 1912, suffragettes led by a Preston woman, Edith Rigby, tarred and feathered the statue after the 16th Earl (son of our statue) strongly opposed votes for women. Though the statue was cleaned, you can still see traces of the incident.

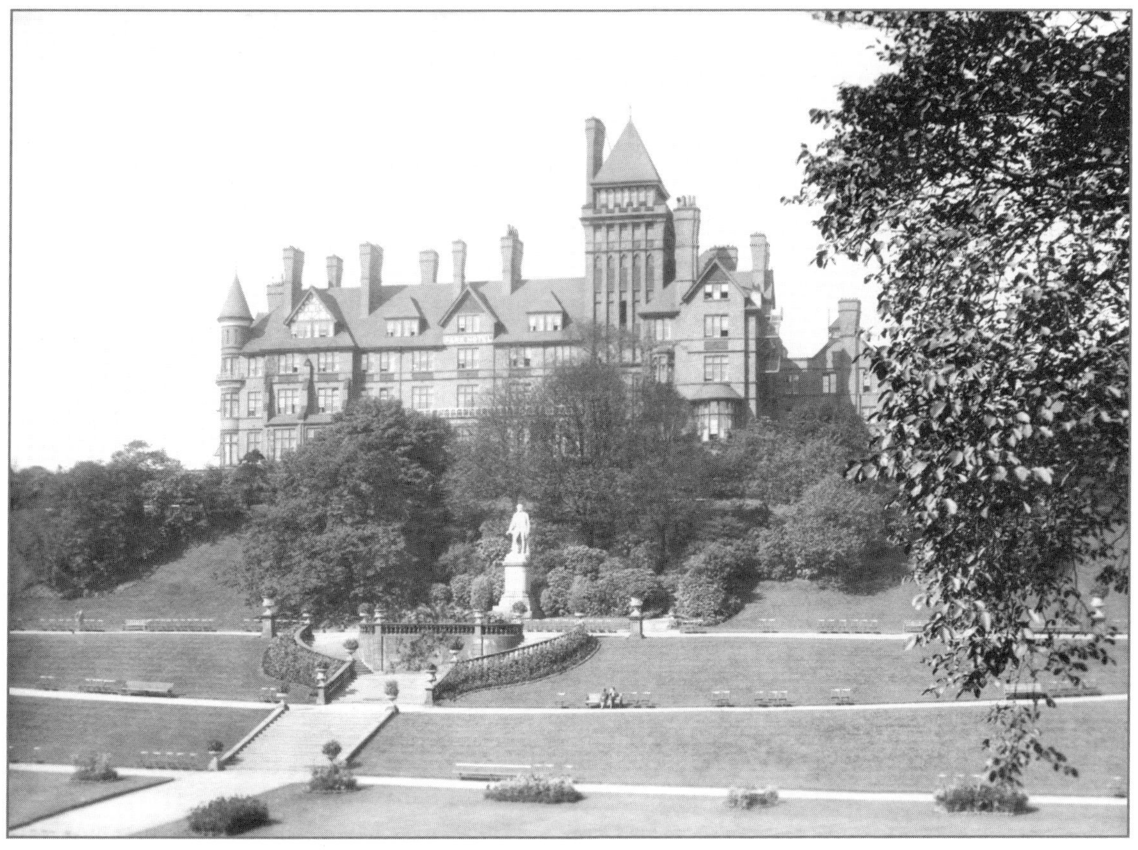

Miller Park 1925 77922
This is a good overall view of the statue of Lord Derby in its magnificent setting, with the Park Hotel behind. The hotel was always slow to modernise, and at the time of this picture it had no bar (was this owing to the T-Total movement in Preston, I wonder?). If guests wanted a drink, they had to have it specially taken to their rooms. Until 1932 hot running water was not available, and anyone wanting a bath would have to telephone down, and again the hot water had to be brought specially to the room. Only the ground floor had central heating, while all the other floors had to rely on coal fires. British Rail sold the building to the County Council in 1950; it was re-vamped, and is now the East Cliff County Offices occupied by the Regional Health Authority.

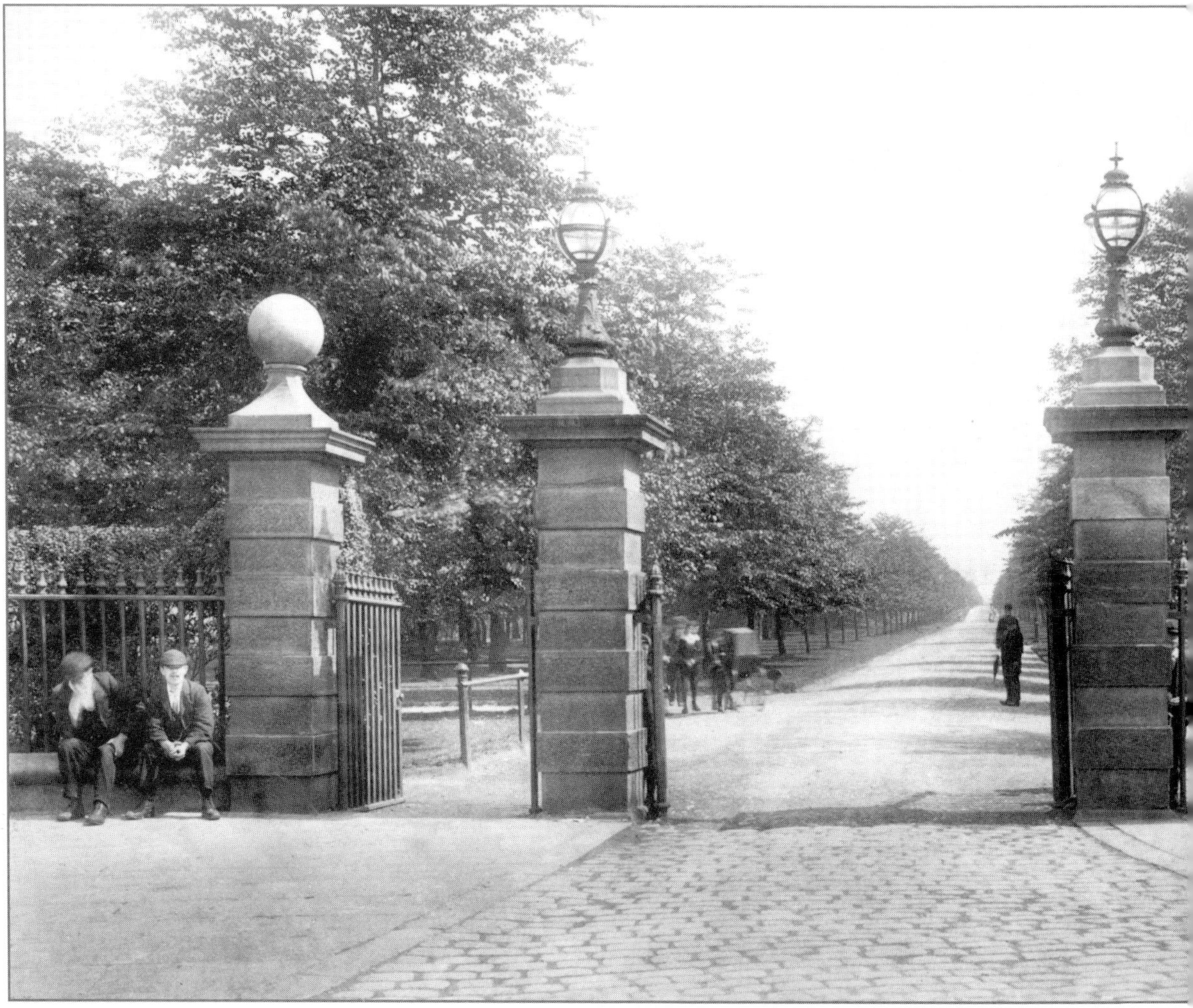

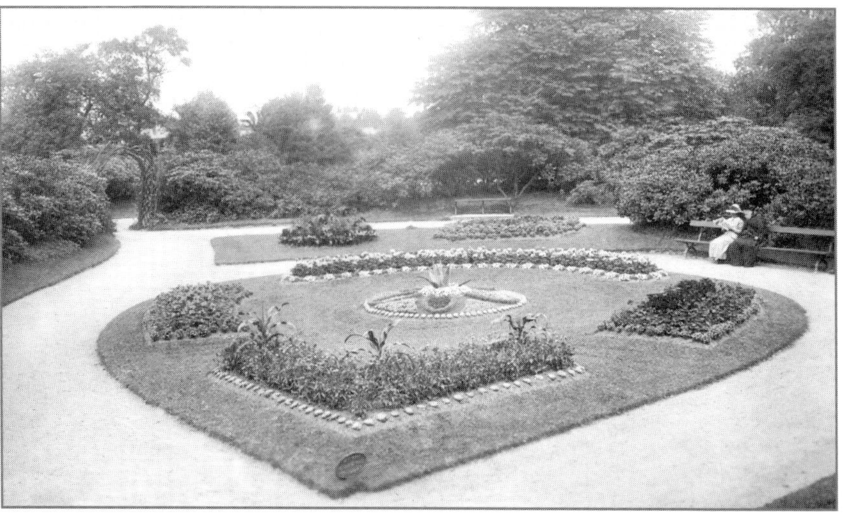

◄ **Moor Park 1913** 65596
Moor Park is actually Preston's oldest open space. At one time any Guild Freeman was allowed to graze cattle here at no charge. The corporation took that right away when they enclosed the area in 1834, and plans for a park were first mentioned a few years later. By 1836 the lake, the Serpentine, had been built, and so had three lodges. It cost £11,000 to drain and level Moor Park and make roads and paths.

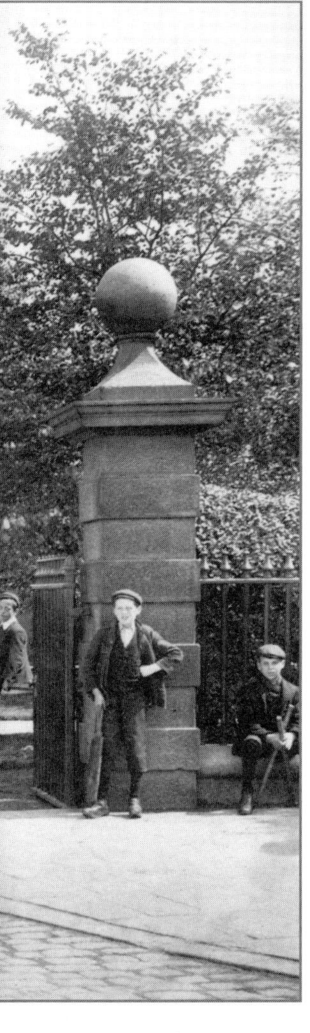

◄ **Moor Park Avenue 1903** 50088
Moor Park, the largest of Preston's parks at 110 acres, lies a mile to the north of the town centre. Here we see the Park's main entrance. Like Preston's two other parks, it was created to provide work for the unemployed, and like Miller and Avenham Parks it was laid out and designed by the London landscape gardener Edward Milner. It was begun in 1864 and opened on 4 October 1867, just one day after the other two parks.

▼ **Moor Park 1924** 75840
Moor Park was always a popular place for children, and I bet our young ladies in the picture had had a smashing time. There was at this time a set of swings for girls and another set for boys, and the playground was also divided. Moor Park had an open-air swimming pool as well. The pool was opened on 7 June 1907 by Alderman Woods. The 32yds by 16yds pool, only 3ft to 4ft 6ins deep, was very popular with the children. It lasted until the early 1970s.

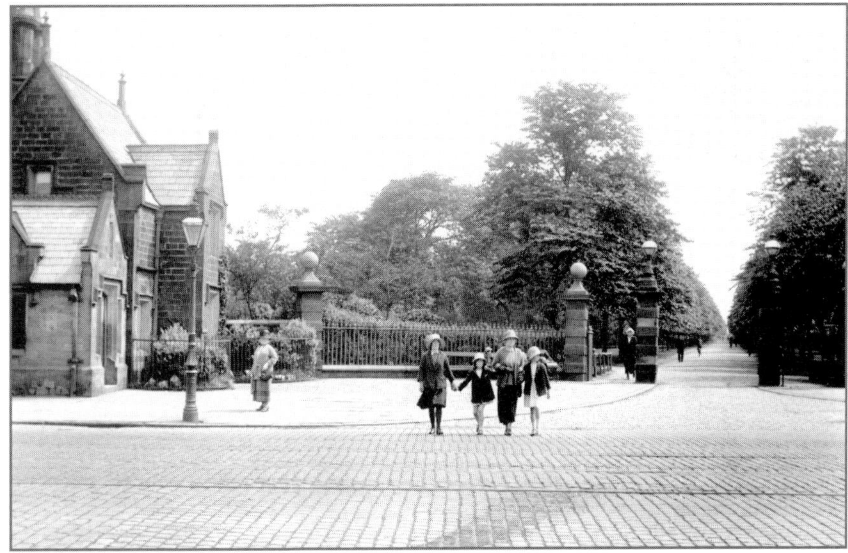

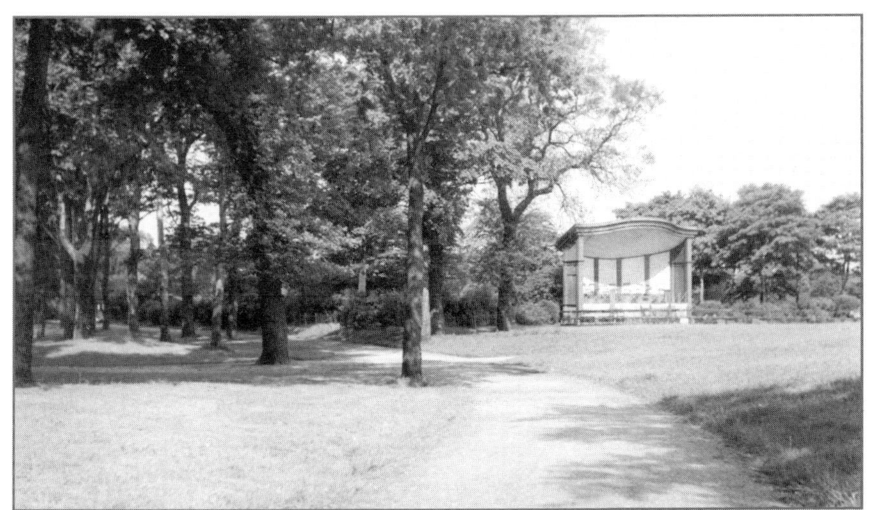

◄ **The Theatre, Moor Park c1960** P113067
This small outdoor theatre was one of many attractions in Moor Park. There was also the Jeremiah Horrocks Observatory and a climatological station for the Air Ministry. The area that is the park today has seen a lot of history. It was here in 1640 that a rally was held to get local people firmly behind the King. In 1648 the Scottish army, hoping to restore Charles I to the throne, camped here on their way south.

Around Preston

The area around Preston is very varied and interesting. The picturesque waterways at Walton contrast with the built-up areas of council estates to the north of Preston, and the large new retail area that was once Preston Docks could not be more different from the lovely unspoilt Ribble Valley leading up to Ribchester and its Roman Fort. The great thing about Preston is that you do not have to travel very far before you are out in lovely Lancashire countryside, or on the Great North Road, the A6, travelling towards Scotland.

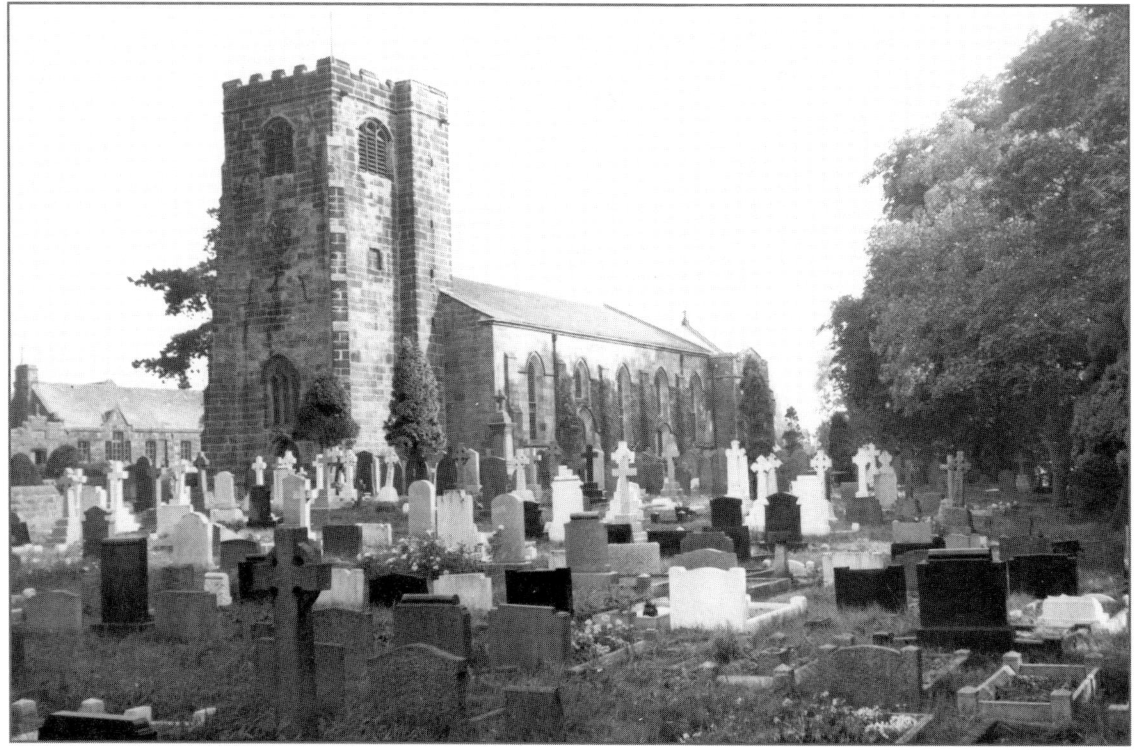

Broughton, The Church c1955 B718001
Broughton is on the Great North Road (the A6), and has managed not to be swallowed up by Preston. Here we see the ancient parish church of St John the Baptist. It is only the tower of this church that is ancient; it dates from the 16th century. Broughton means 'the place by the brook'. The brook that gave it its name was Woodplumpton Brook, which runs past Broughton House.

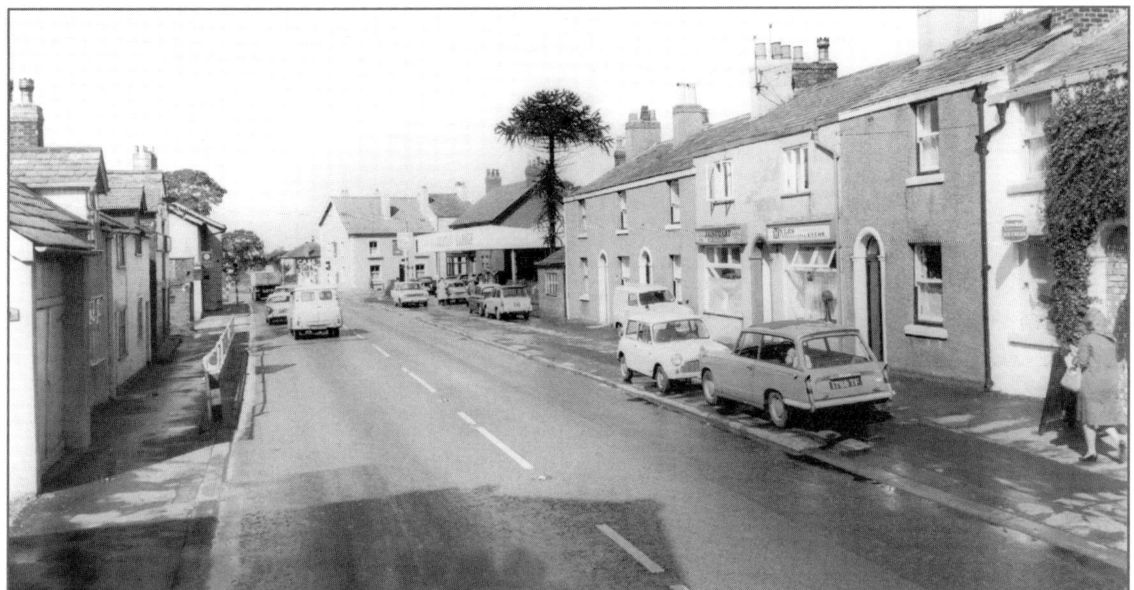

Broughton, The High Street c1965 B718010
The High Street may look quiet and rural, but five years earlier this street was pounded with traffic day and night. The cars parked on the pavement gives a hint of the traffic problems caused by people heading to the Lakes or southwards. In the summer time and on Bank Holidays, you could be an hour just getting through this mile-long village. The Preston by-pass opened in 1959, and the motorway from junction 32 near Broughton to junction 33 at Hampson Green opened six years later. That gave the villagers a little of their peace back.

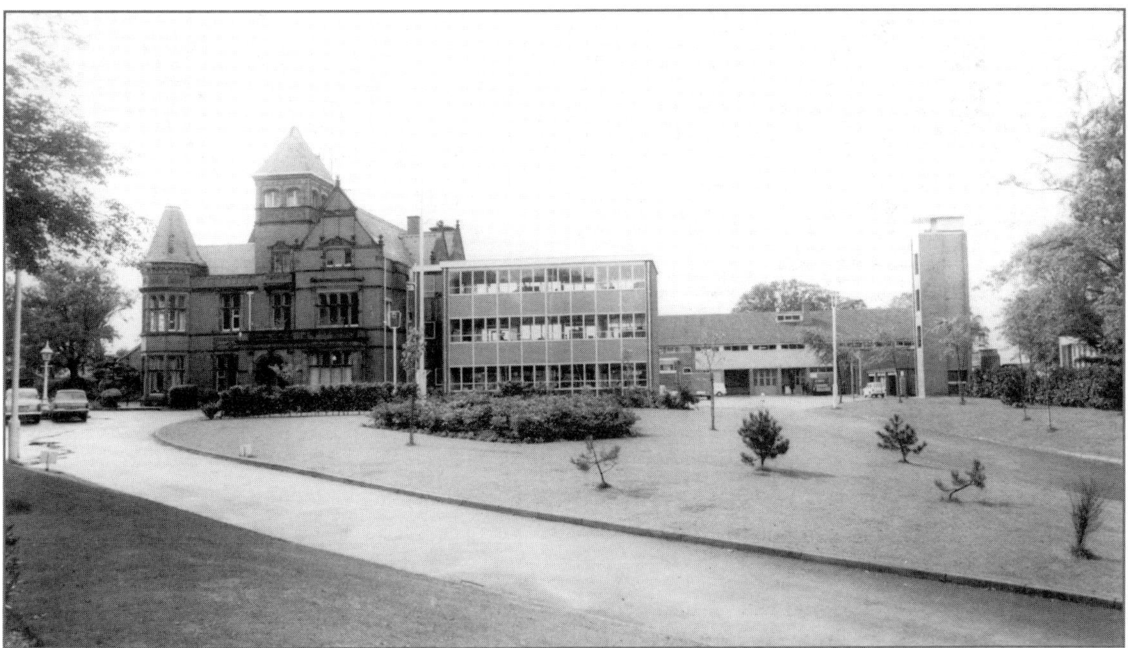

Broughton, Fire Brigade HQ c1965 B718006
Preston is a County Borough, and so it needed a new HQ for the County Fire Brigade. Traffic played a large part in the decision to site the new Headquarters out at Broughton, which we see here just after it opened. There are five or six main roads into Preston from here, and if roads are blocked with holiday traffic there are always alternatives.

Balderstone, St Leonard's Church c1955 B852011
Balderstone can be found a few miles up the Ribble Valley from Preston, just half way to Ribchester. The name comes from an Old English personal name, and was first mentioned in 1280. Here we see the parish church of St Leonard's, complete with spire and lych gate.

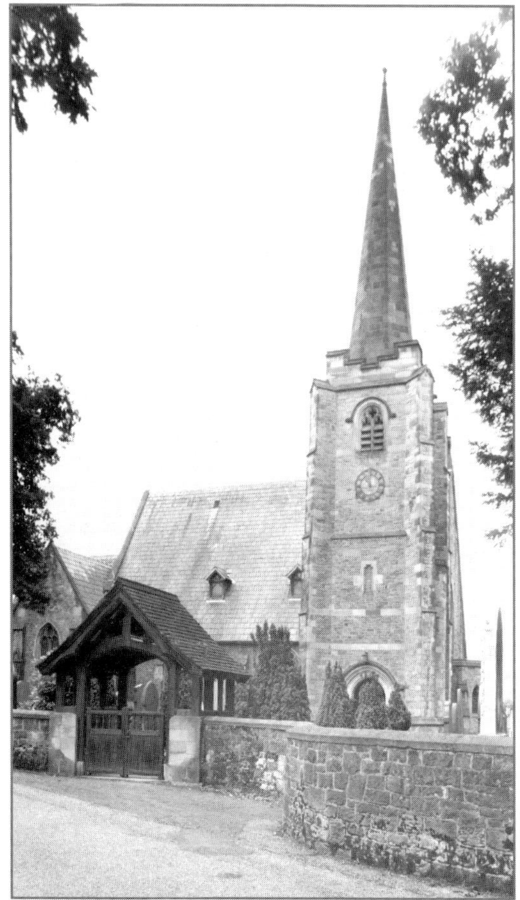

Farington, Stanifield Lane c1955 F223003
This is another view of Stanifield Lane, but further out from the village. The pre-war houses stand neat and square on the lane. Farington is a parish in Preston Rural District.

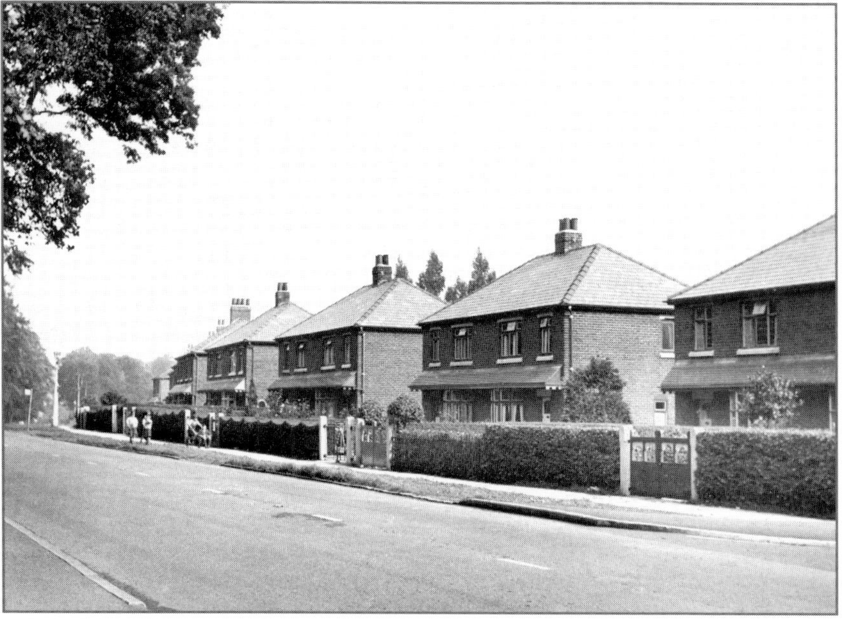

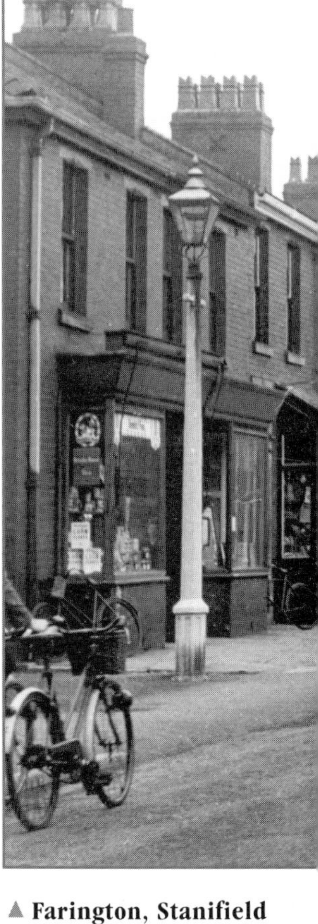

Farington, Stanifield Lane c1955 F223006
Stanifield Lane is one of the two main roads that go through Farington, which is south of Preston and roughly half-way to Leyland. This photograph reflects the innocence and simplicity of the 1950s: note the gate post with an advertisement painted on it, the motor bike and sidecar, bikes with shopping baskets and the lady with rollers and scarf just nipping out to the corner shop.

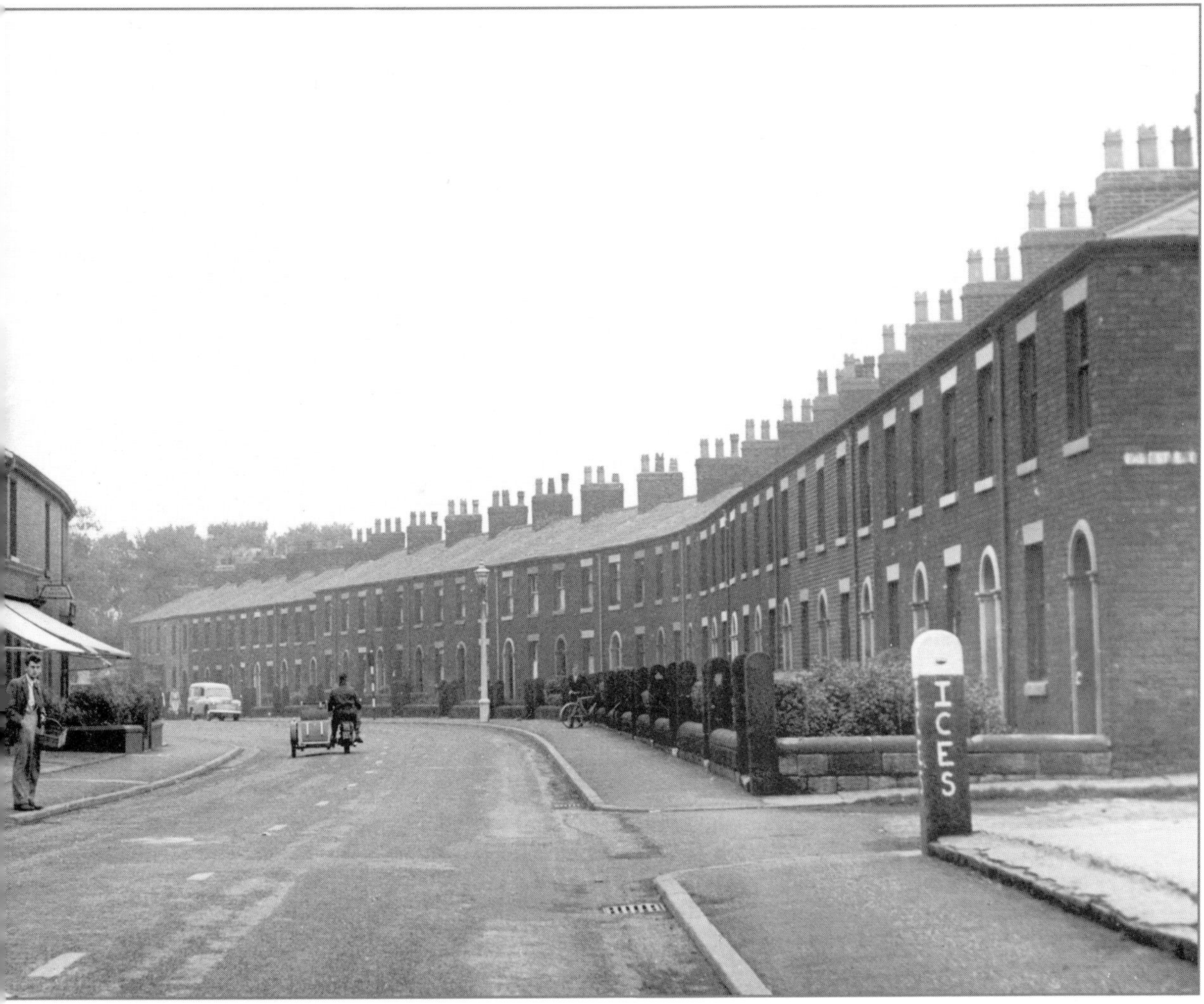

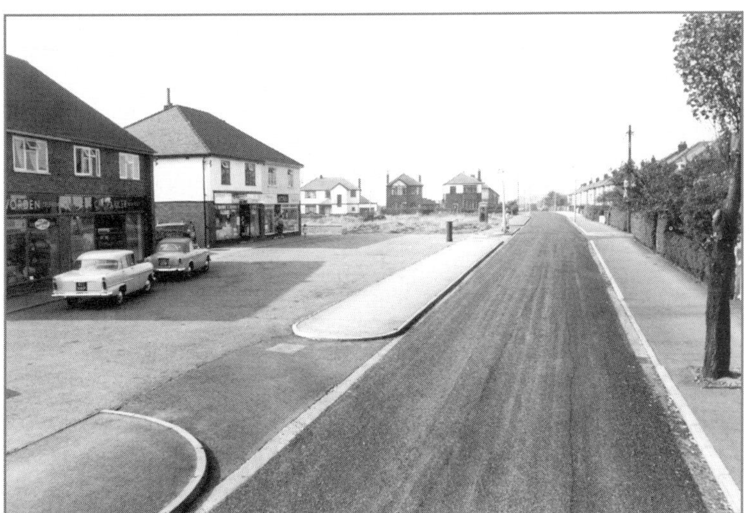

◄ **Fulwood**
Beech Drive c1965 F198015

Fulwood is north of Preston, sitting astride the A6, the Great North Road. It was an Urban District in its own right. Our photograph of Beech Drive shows how the area was, mainly residential. At the time of this photograph there were more than 18,000 people living in the 33,164 acres - 2,400 houses were built here between 1945 and 1965. This area was the site of part of the Battle of Ribbleton Moor, and cannon balls and bones were found here more than once while all that building was going on.

▼ **Fulwood, The Methodist Church c1965** F198002

The name Fulwood comes from the Old English and means 'dirty or foul wood'. Here we see the main road leading north from Preston and the Methodist Church. The Harris Orphanage was built out here in 1888 so that the children could benefit from the fresh country air away from the grimy town.

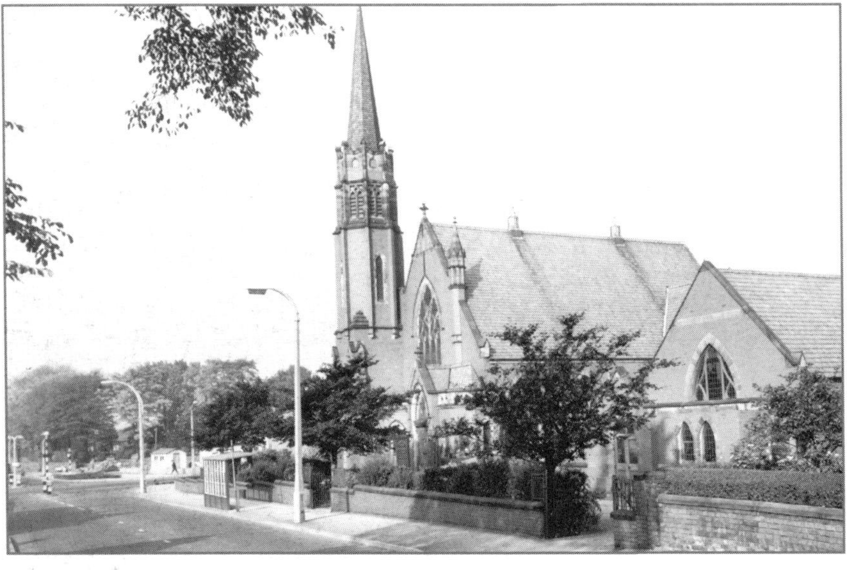

▼ **Longridge, Market Place c1955** L340006

Longridge stands about six miles from Preston on the Clitheroe Road. It still shows many of the signs of a country village, and is complete with its Market Square, as our photograph shows. Longridge takes its name from being at the end of Longridge Fell. The Dog Inn is on the right, and Sanderson the Butcher is across the road on the corner.

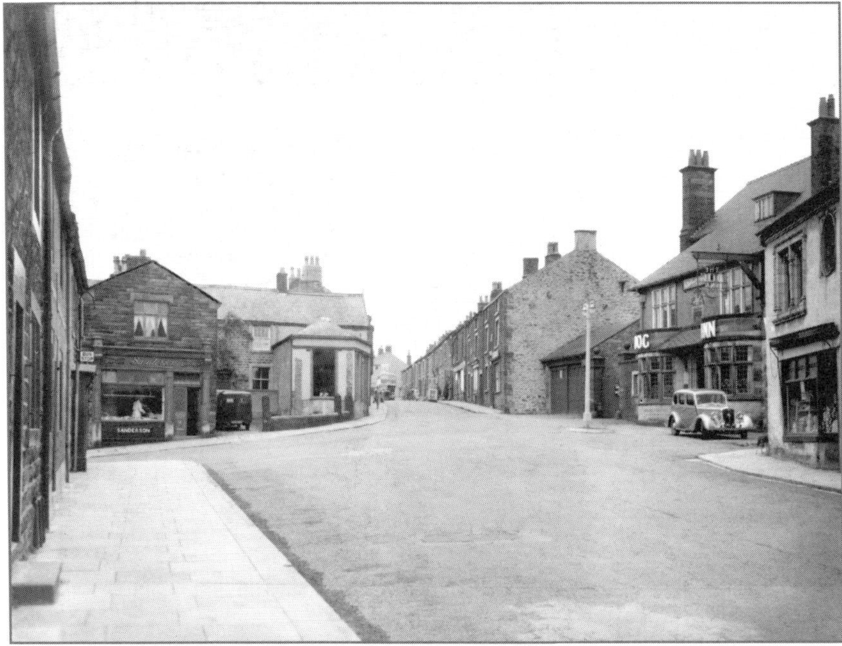

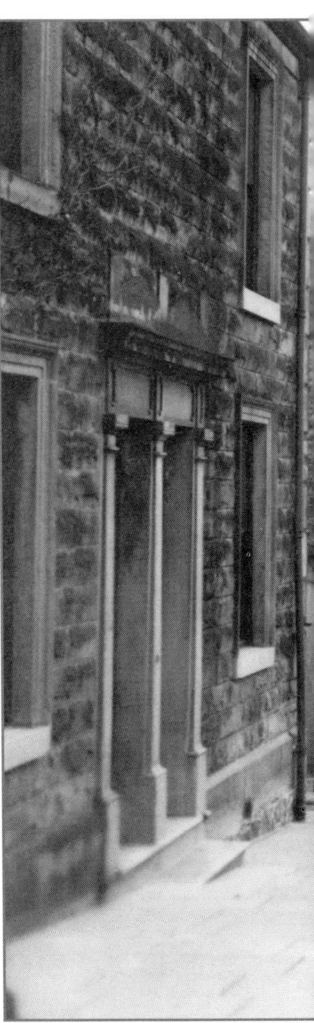

▲ **Longridge, Berry Lane c1955** L340004

We are looking down Berry Lane back towards Preston. Longridge was an Urban District Council; it comprised 3,285 acres, and when this photograph was taken had around 5,320 people living in the area, which included Alston and Dilworth.

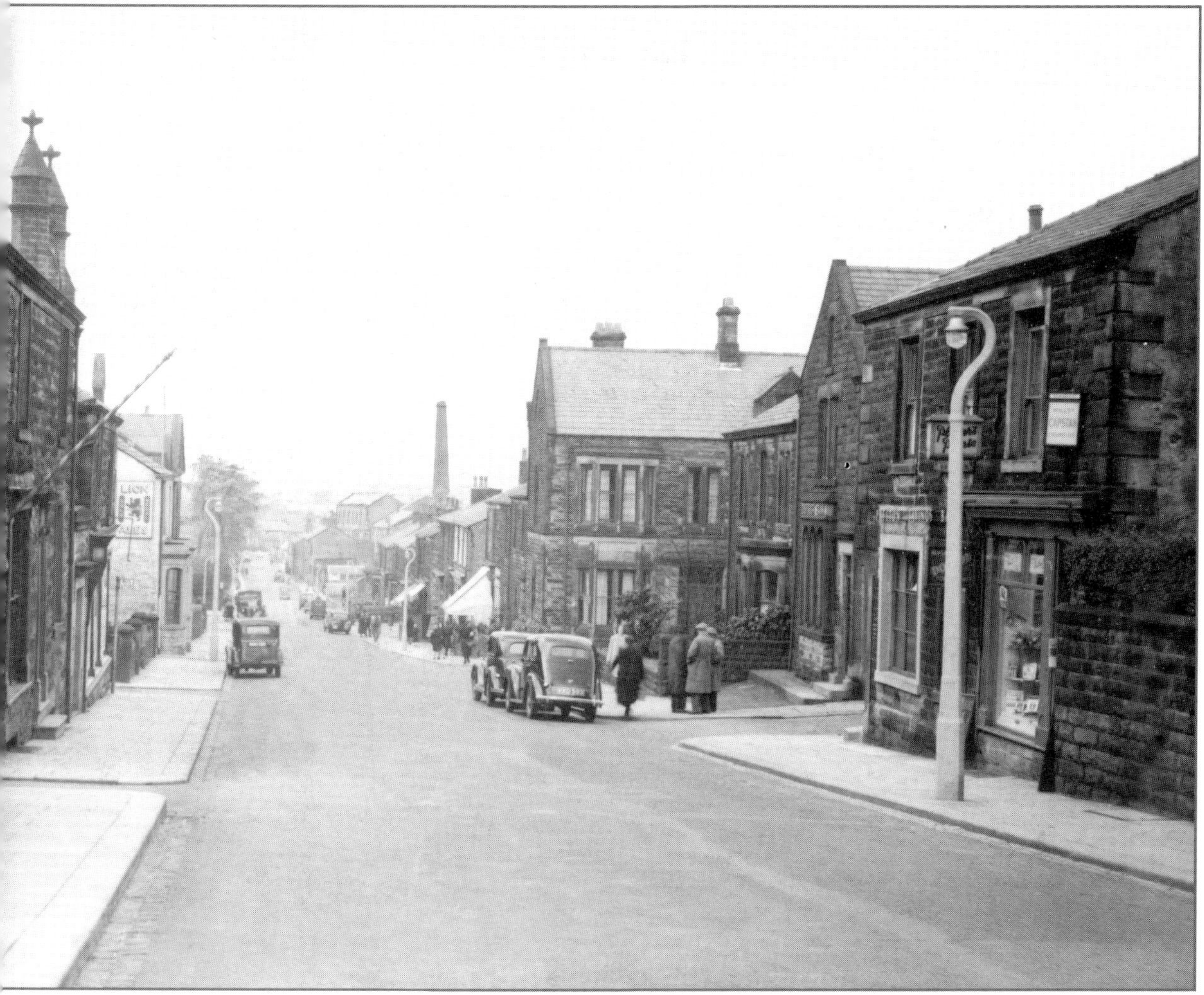

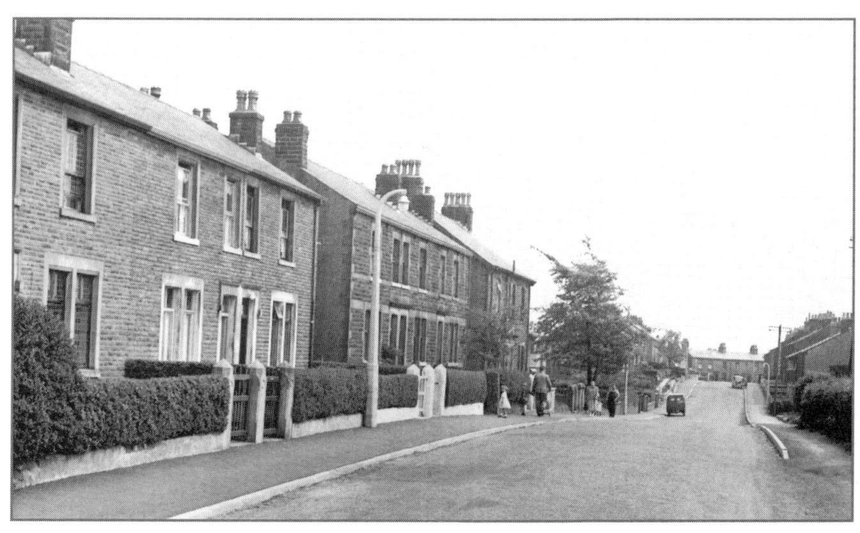

◄ **Longridge, Little Lane c1955** L340014
Here we see a quiet rural scene in a typical Lancashire village. The village had three churches at the time, and two unusual wayside monuments.

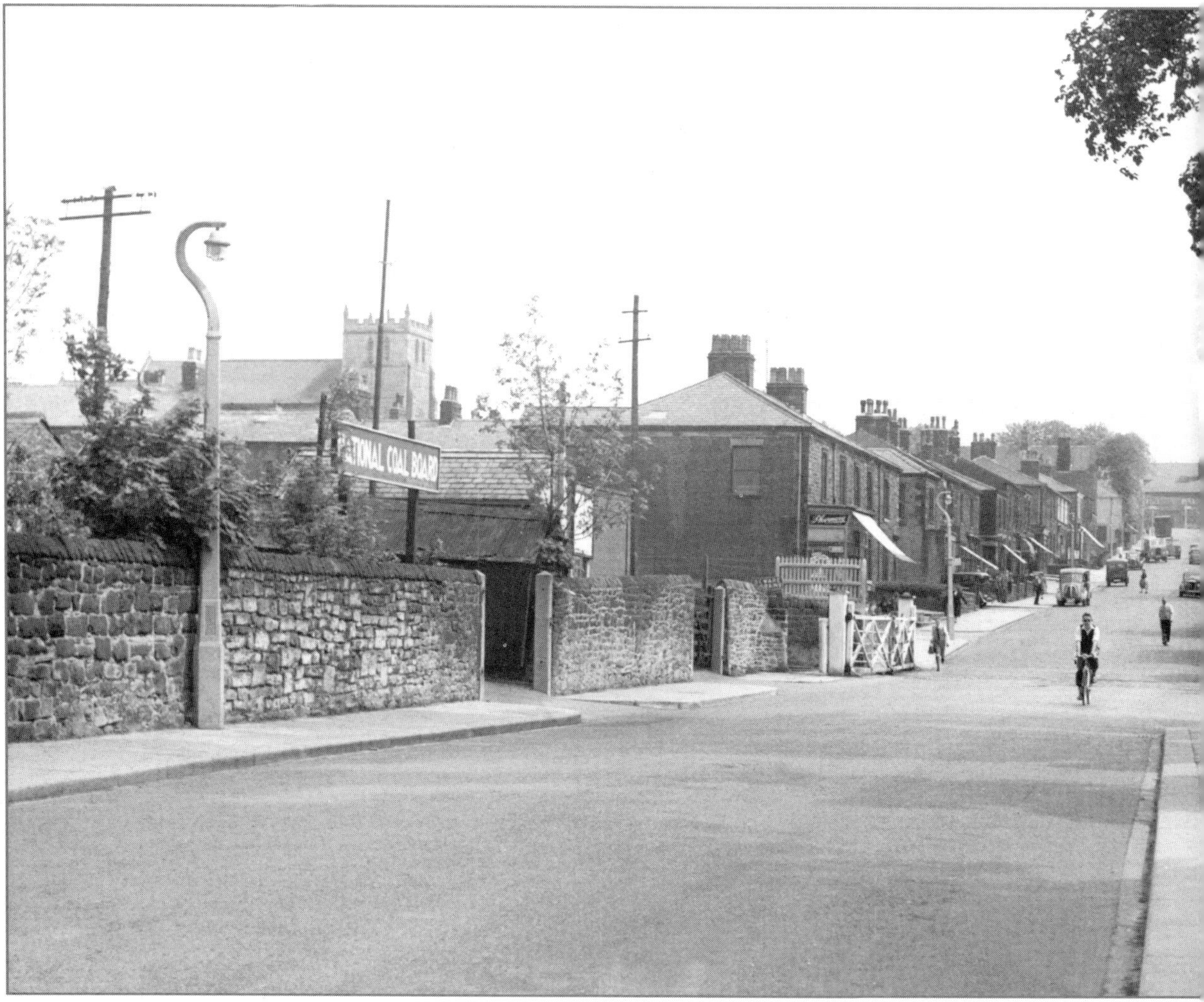

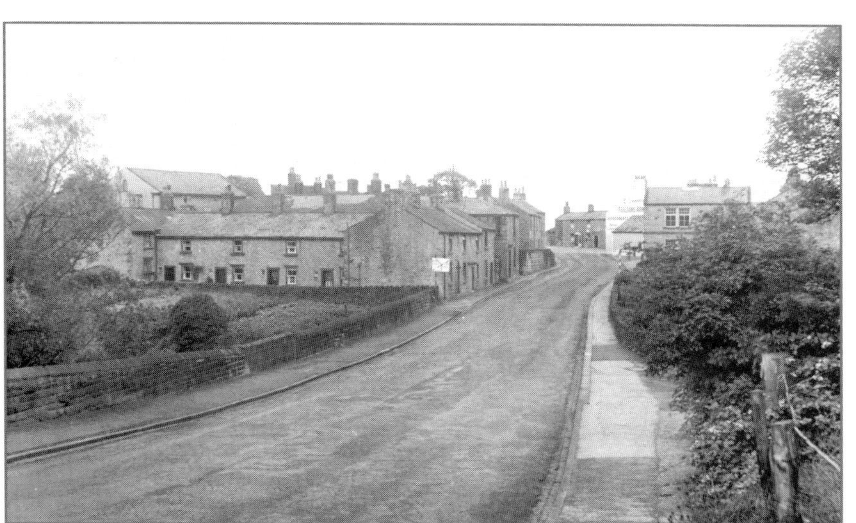

Mellor Brook, Whalley Road c1955 M309002
Mellor Brook is just six miles from Preston and near the ancient village of Mellor. Here we see the A49 road through Mellor Brook; today there is a new road taking traffic away from the village. You can just see the road sign warning of the splits in the road ahead, and the inn at the top of the hill.

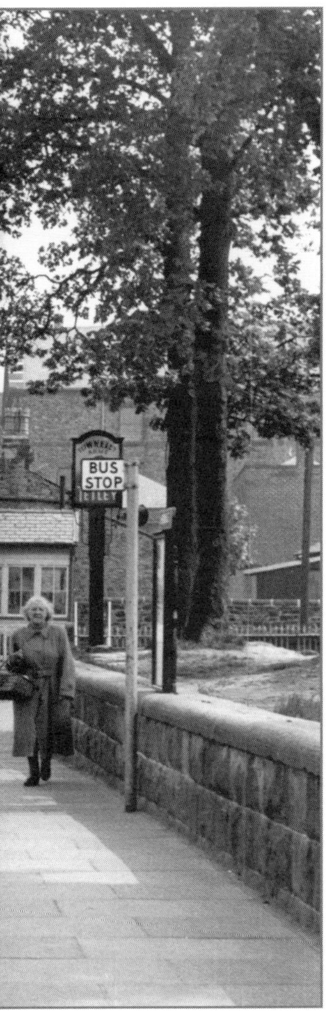

Longridge, Berry Lane c1955 L340012
This view shows the level crossing at the bottom of Berry Lane. There is a National Coal Board Depot on the left, and just above the sign we can see the tower of the parish church, St Lawrence's. The tower was built in 1841. Many of the shops have their blinds out, so it cannot be a Wednesday - that was half-day closing.

Mellor Brook, The Village c1955 M309001
We are looking towards the centre of Mellor Brook. The Feilden's Arms, seen at the top of the hill in the photograph at the bottom of the previous page is on the left. As we can see from the advertisements on the wall, it sold C & S Blackpool Ales, and the landlord was Mr J Kay; he also sold teas, snacks and ices.

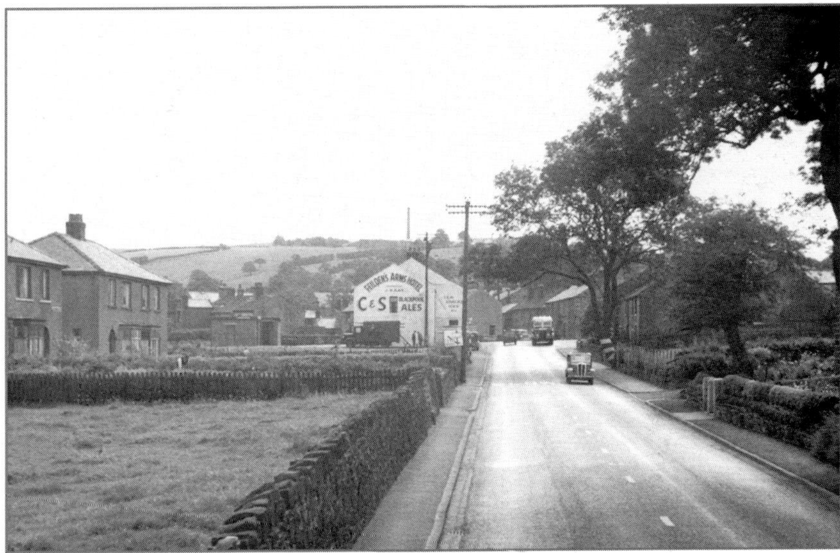

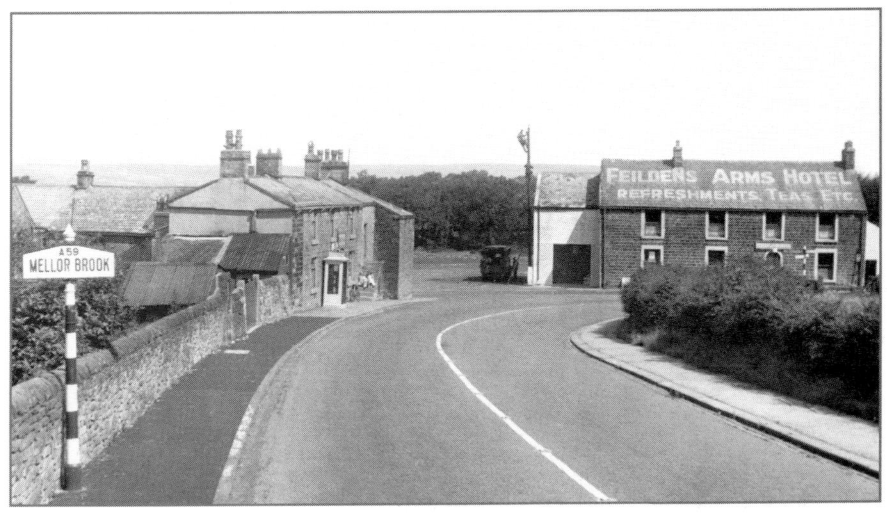

Mellor Brook The Post Office c1955 M309010
This is the A49, and we can see the Feilden's Arms head on. Because Samlesbury Hall was so near, the area was popular with walkers and day trippers in the post-war years. You can see the local post office on the left of the road with a telephone box outside.

Penwortham The Church and the Lych Gate 1903 50075

The very ancient settlement of Penwortham lies over on the south bank of the Ribble. Roger de Poitou, the Norman knight who was given most of Lancashire, built a large castle here, but all that remains of it today is the name Castle Hill. The place was mentioned in the Domesday Book, and in 1140 it was spelt 'Pennerthan'. The name means 'the enclosed homestead on the hill'.

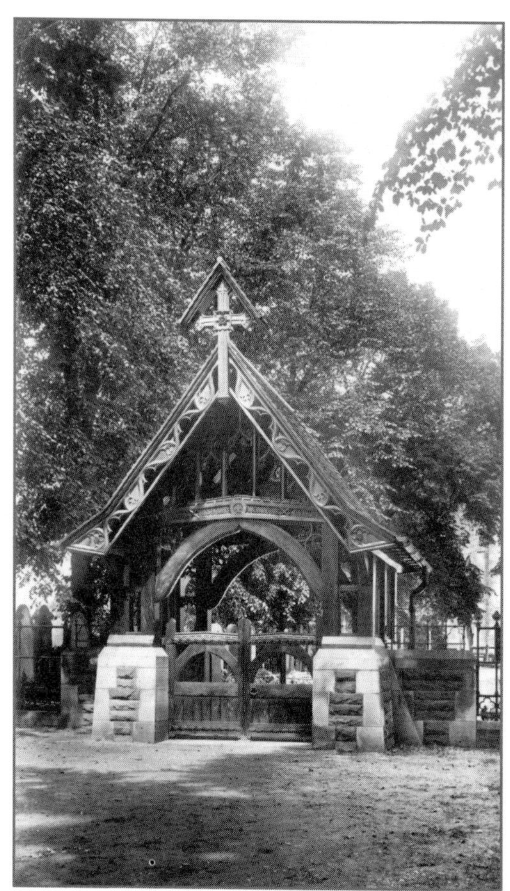

Penwortham The Church 1893 33102

Here we have a lovely view of St Mary's, the parish church of Penwortham. The most famous person resting here must be John Horrocks, who founded his great cotton empire at Preston. You can see the iron railings around his grave at the bottom left of our picture. The church is built in Perpendicular style.

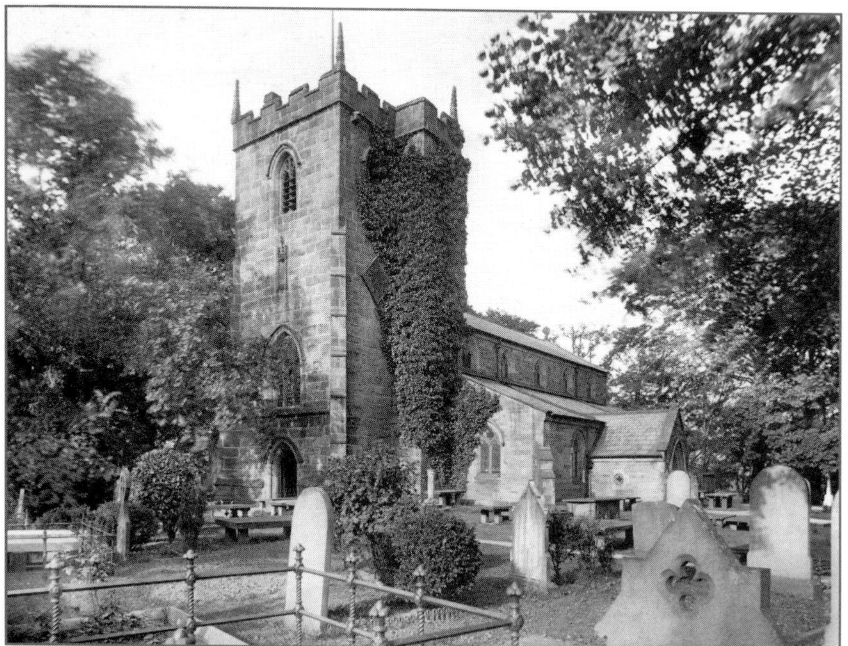

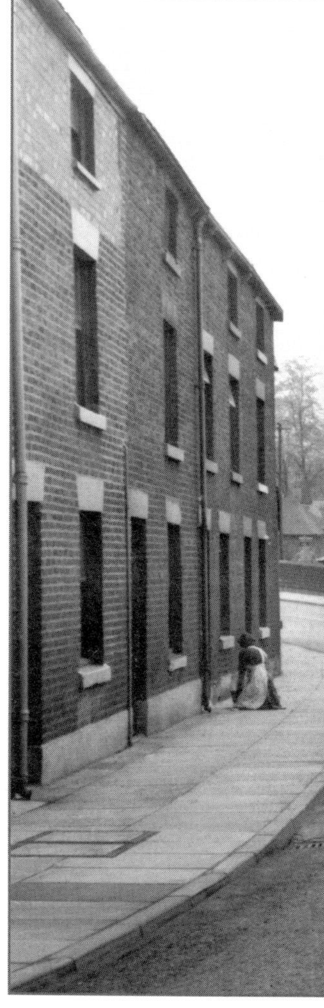

Walton-le-Dale The Old Unicorn Chorley Road c1955

W524002

The Old Unicorn Inn lies at the centre of Walton-le-Dale. The inn also had a dining room and tea rooms. It was in this area in 1648 that Cromwell made his headquarters, and he is reputed to have stayed at the Old Unicorn.

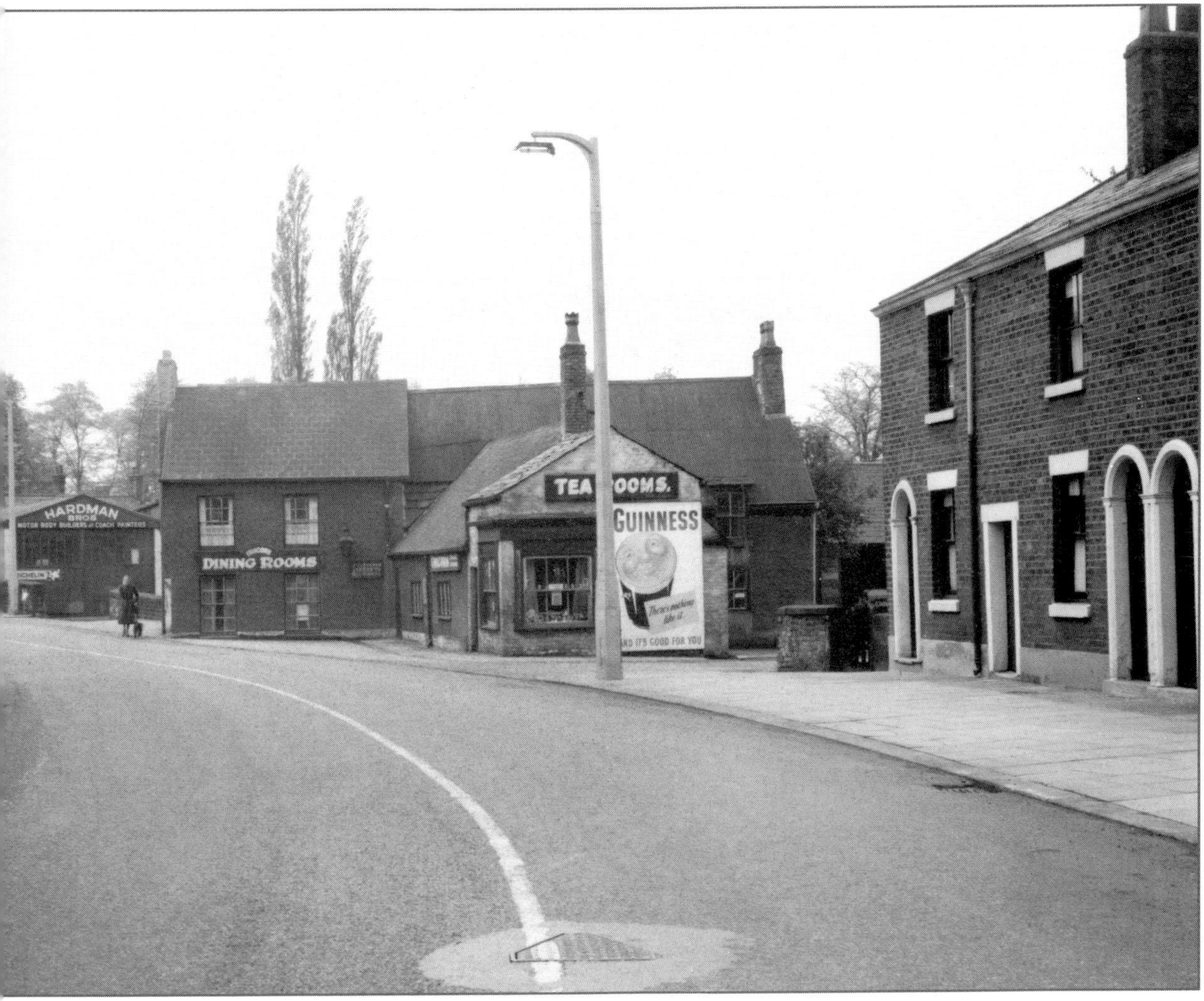

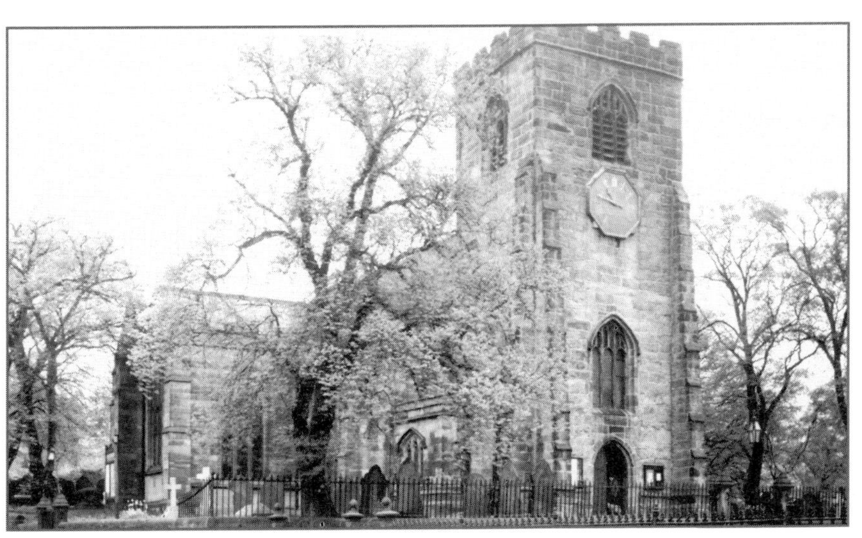

◄ **Walton-le-Dale St Leonard's church c1955** W524006
This parish church, situated in Cuerdale Lane, is more or less unchanged since the 17th century. In Roman times, Walton-le-Dale was known as Rigodunum, and in Saxon times it was called Waelletune. The manor was granted to Robert Bannastre by Henry de Lacy in the 12th century.

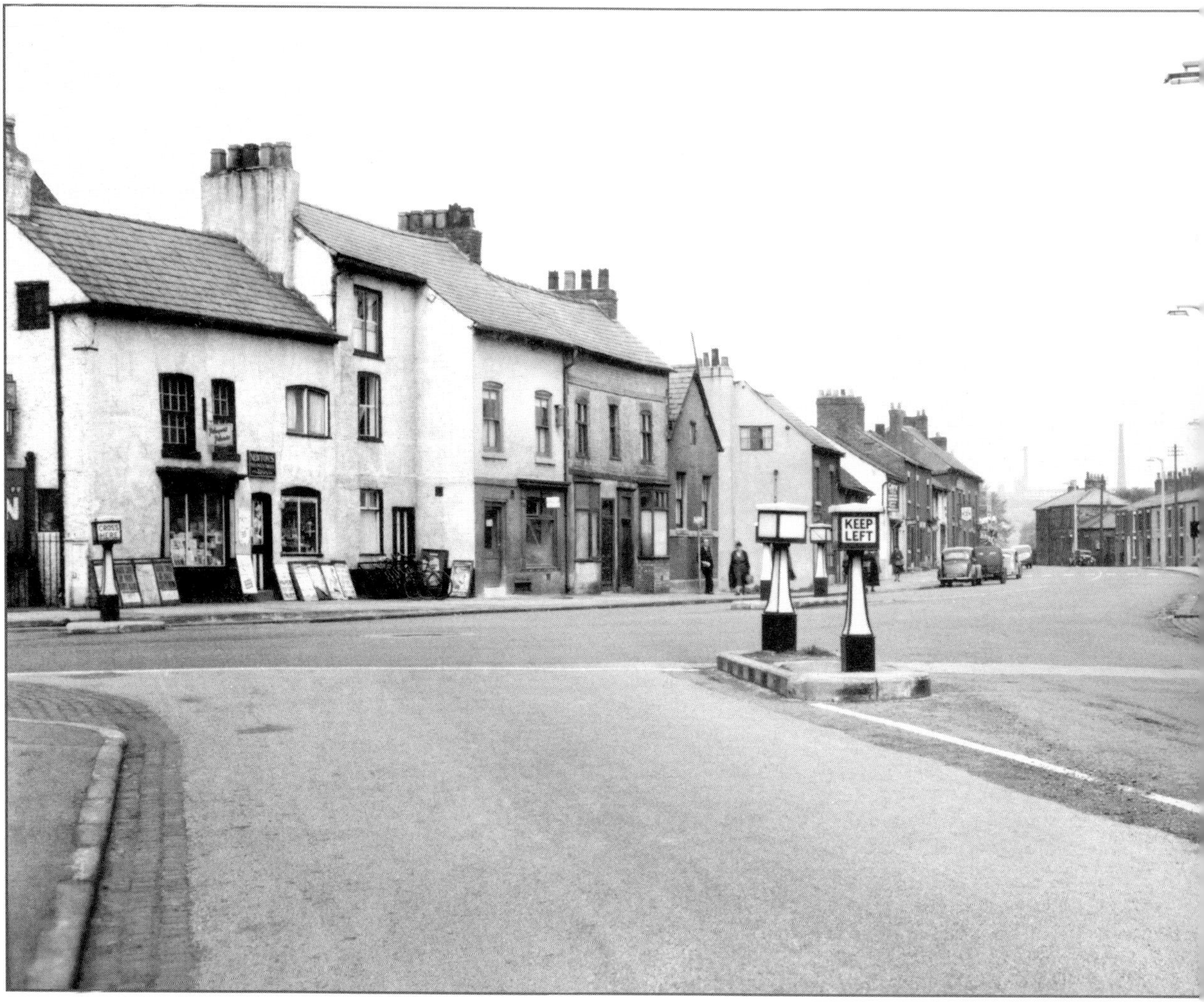

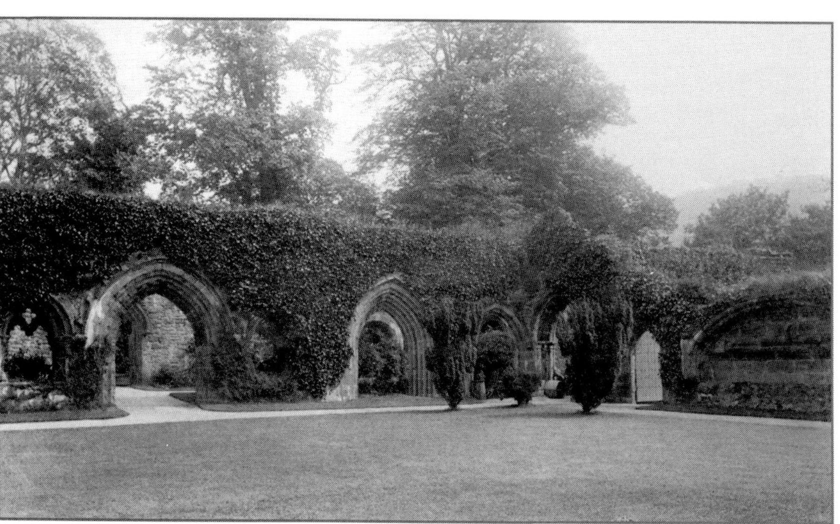

◄ **Whalley, The Abbey Cloister 1894** 34332
Whalley is a very ancient town and steeped in history. The Abbey was begun in the 12th century, and its ruins (seen here ivy-covered, as they used to be) have been a place to visit for over three hundred years. The church at Whalley is equally interesting, and it has a St Cuthbert Cross in the churchyard.

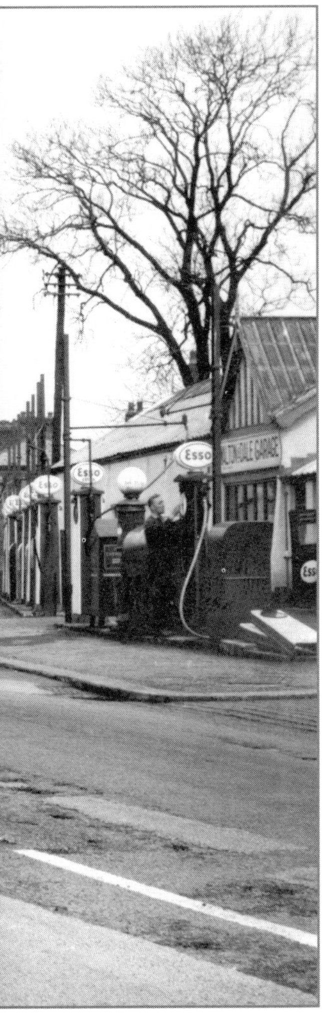

◄ **Walton-le-Dale, Victoria Road c1955** W524005

This view shows the main road through Walton-le-Dale. Walton-le-Dale Urban District included Higher Walton, Gregson Lane, Bamber Bridge and Lostock Hall as well as Walton itself. Victoria Road was part of the A6; it was constructed along the line of the old Roman Road that went through here.

▼ **Hoghton Tower 1895**

35719

The driveway up to the Tower is as long and straight as a Roman road. Built by the de Hoghton family at the time of Queen Elizabeth I, the tower is built around two courtyards. The house is historically very interesting, and there are many mysterious tales about it.

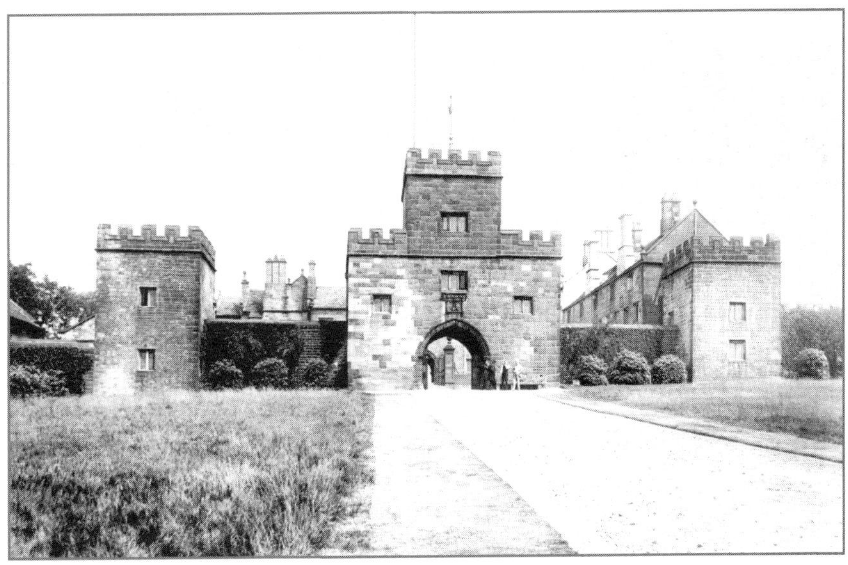

◄ **Stoneyhurst The College 1899**

43487

This unusual view of Stoneyhurst College shows the chapel on the left. There are many articles of interest from the past kept at the school, including Mary Queen of Scots' book of hours and Bonny Prince Charlie's flask. The College is open to visitors every summer, and is well worth the effort to see.

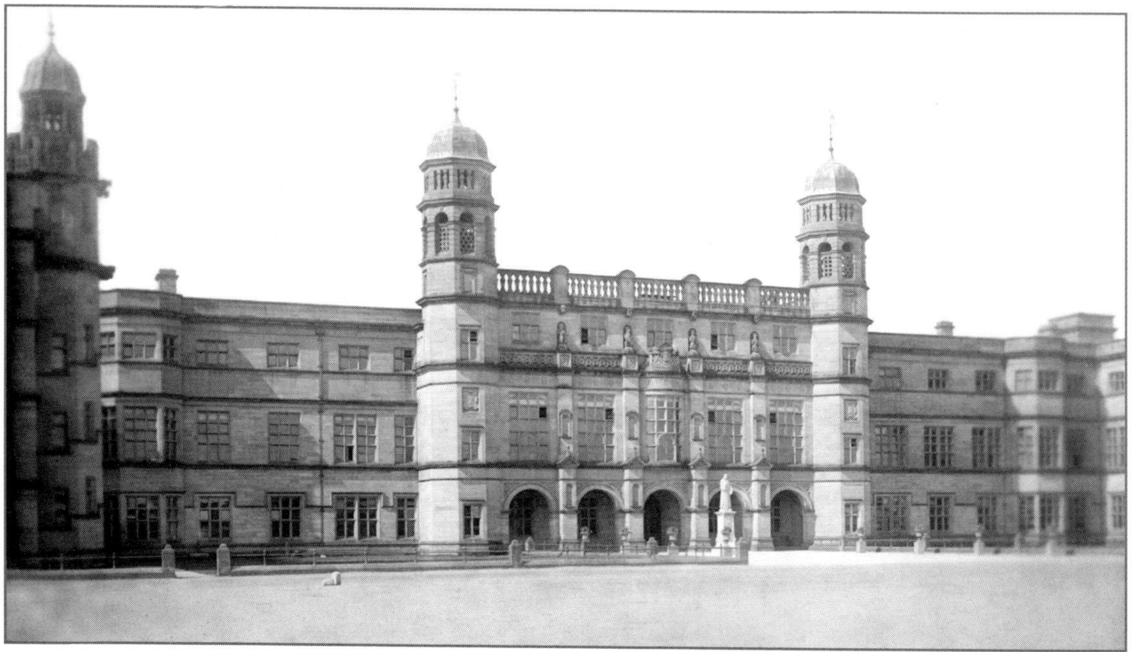

Stoneyhurst, The College 1893 33105
Here we see the back of the college. The Shireburn family lie in the ancient church of Mitton just a few miles away from the College. The Shireburn family's daughter married the Duke of Norfolk; she returned to give her family members buried in the chapel grand memorials.

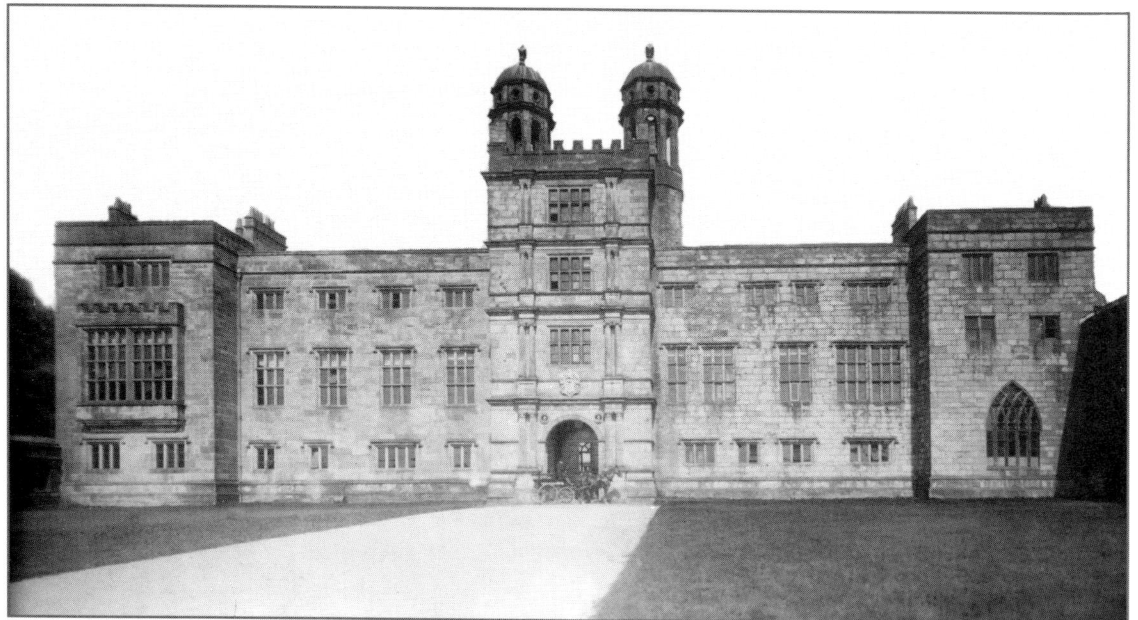

Stoneyhurst, The College from the West 1893 33104
Built as Stoneyhurst Hall by Sir Richard Shireburn, the building was abandoned by the family and given to the Catholic Church; it became a school run by Jesuit Priests. Stoneyhurst College had a reputation which spread all over the world, and its former pupils included the actor Charles Laughton and Conan Doyle, the creator of Sherlock Holmes.

Index

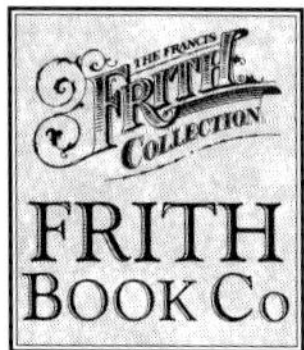

Frith Book Co Titles

www.frithbook.co.uk

The Frith Book Company publishes over 100 new titles each year. A selection of those currently available are listed below. For latest catalogue please contact Frith Book Co.

Town Books 96pp, 100 photos. County and Themed Books 128pp, 150 photos (unless specified). All titles hardback laminated case and jacket except those indicated pb (paperback)

Around Bakewell	1-85937-113-2	£12.99
Around Barnstaple	1-85937-084-5	£12.99
Around Bath	1-85937-097-7	£12.99
Berkshire (pb)	1-85937-191-4	£9.99
Around Blackpool	1-85937-049-7	£12.99
Around Bognor Regis	1-85937-055-1	£12.99
Around Bournemouth	1-85937-067-5	£12.99
Brighton (pb)	1-85937-192-2	£8.99
British Life A Century Ago	1-85937-103-5	£17.99
Buckinghamshire (pb)	1-85937-200-7	£9.99
Around Cambridge	1-85937-092-6	£12.99
Cambridgeshire	1-85937-086-1	£14.99
Canals and Waterways	1-85937-129-9	£17.99
Cheshire	1-85937-045-4	£14.99
Around Chester	1-85937-090-x	£12.99
Around Chichester	1-85937-089-6	£12.99
Churches of Berkshire	1-85937-170-1	£17.99
Churches of Dorset	1-85937-172-8	£17.99
Colchester (pb)	1-85937-188-4	£8.99
Cornwall	1-85937-054-3	£14.99
Cumbria	1-85937-101-9	£14.99
Dartmoor	1-85937-145-0	£14.99
Around Derby	1-85937-046-2	£12.99
Derbyshire (pb)	1-85937-196-5	£9.99
Devon	1-85937-052-7	£14.99
Dorset	1-85937-075-6	£14.99
Dorset Coast	1-85937-062-4	£14.99
Down the Severn	1-85937-118-3	£14.99
Down the Thames	1-85937-121-3	£14.99
Around Dublin	1-85937-058-6	£12.99
East Sussex	1-85937-130-2	£14.99
Around Eastbourne	1-85937-061-6	£12.99
Edinburgh (pb)	1-85937-193-0	£8.99
English Castles	1-85937-078-0	£14.99
Essex	1-85937-082-9	£14.99
Around Exeter	1-85937-126-4	£12.99
Exmoor	1-85937-132-9	£14.99
Around Falmouth	1-85937-066-7	£12.99
Around Great Yarmouth	1-85937-085-3	£12.99
Around Guildford	1-85937-117-5	£12.99
Hampshire	1-85937-064-0	£14.99
Around Harrogate	1-85937-112-4	£12.99
Around Horsham	1-85937-127-2	£12.99
Around Ipswich	1-85937-133-7	£12.99
Ireland (pb)	1-85937-181-7	£9.99
Isle of Man	1-85937-065-9	£14.99
Isle of Wight	1-85937-114-0	£14.99
Kent (pb)	1-85937-189-2	£9.99
Around Leicester	1-85937-073-x	£12.99
Leicestershire (pb)	1-85937-185-x	£9.99
Around Lincoln	1-85937-111-6	£12.99
Lincolnshire	1-85937-135-3	£14.99
London (pb)	1-85937-183-3	£9.99
Around Maidstone	1-85937-056-x	£12.99
New Forest	1-85937-128-0	£14.99
Around Newark	1-85937-105-1	£12.99
Around Newquay	1-85937-140-x	£12.99
North Devon Coast	1-85937-146-9	£14.99
Northumberland and Tyne & Wear	1-85937-072-1	£14.99
Norwich (pb)	1-85937-194-9	£8.99
Around Nottingham	1-85937-060-8	£12.99
Nottinghamshire (pb)	1-85937-187-6	£9.99
Around Oxford	1-85937-096-9	£12.99
Oxfordshire	1-85937-076-4	£14.99
Peak District	1-85937-100-0	£14.99
Around Penzance	1-85937-069-1	£12.99
Around Plymouth	1-85937-119-1	£12.99
Around St Ives	1-85937-068-3	£12.99
Around Scarborough	1-85937-104-3	£12.99
Scotland (pb)	1-85937-182-5	£9.99
Scottish Castles	1-85937-077-2	£14.99
Around Sevenoaks and Tonbridge	1-85937-057-8	£12.99
Around Southampton	1-85937-088-8	£12.99
Around Southport	1-85937-106-x	£12.99

Available from your local bookshop or from the publisher

Frith Book Co Titles (continued)

Around Shrewsbury	1-85937-110-8	£12.99
Shropshire	1-85937-083-7	£14.99
South Devon Coast	1-85937-107-8	£14.99
South Devon Living Memories	1-85937-168-x	£14.99
Staffordshire (96pp)	1-85937-047-0	£12.99
Stone Circles & Ancient Monuments	1-85937-143-4	£17.99
Around Stratford upon Avon	1-85937-098-5	£12.99
Sussex (pb)	1-85937-184-1	£9.99
Around Torbay	1-85937-063-2	£12.99
Around Truro	1-85937-147-7	£12.99
Victorian & Edwardian Kent	1-85937-149-3	£14.99
Victorian & Edwardian Yorkshire	1-85937-154-x	£14.99
Warwickshire (pb)	1-85937-203-1	£9.99
Welsh Castles	1-85937-120-5	£14.99
West Midlands	1-85937-109-4	£14.99
West Sussex	1-85937-148-5	£14.99
Wiltshire	1-85937-053-5	£14.99
Around Winchester	1-85937-139-6	£12.99

Frith Book Co titles available Autumn 2000

Croydon Living Memories (pb)	1-85937-162-0	£9.99	Aug
Glasgow (pb)	1-85937-190-6	£9.99	Aug
Hertfordshire (pb)	1-85937-247-3	£9.99	Aug
North London	1-85937-206-6	£14.99	Aug
Victorian & Edwardian Maritime Album	1-85937-144-2	£17.99	Aug
Victorian Seaside	1-85937-159-0	£17.99	Aug
Cornish Coast	1-85937-163-9	£14.99	Sep
County Durham	1-85937-123-x	£14.99	Sep
Dorset Living Memories	1-85937-210-4	£14.99	Sep
Herefordshire	1-85937-174-4	£14.99	Sep
Kent Living Memories	1-85937-125-6	£14.99	Sep
Leeds (pb)	1-85937-202-3	£9.99	Sep
Ludlow (pb)	1-85937-176-0	£9.99	Sep
Norfolk (pb)	1-85937-195-7	£9.99	Sep
Somerset	1-85937-153-1	£14.99	Sep
Tees Valley & Cleveland	1-85937-211-2	£14.99	Sep
Thanet (pb)	1-85937-116-7	£9.99	Sep
Tiverton (pb)	1-85937-178-7	£9.99	Sep
Victorian and Edwardian Sussex	1-85937-157-4	£14.99	Sep
Weymouth (pb)	1-85937-209-0	£9.99	Sep
Worcestershire	1-85937-152-3	£14.99	Sep
Yorkshire Living Memories	1-85937-166-3	£14.99	Sep
British Life A Century Ago (pb)	1-85937-213-9	£9.99	Oct
Camberley (pb)	1-85937-222-8	£9.99	Oct
Cardiff (pb)	1-85937-093-4	£9.99	Oct
Carmarthenshire	1-85937-216-3	£14.99	Oct
Cornwall (pb)	1-85937-229-5	£9.99	Oct
English Country Houses	1-85937-161-2	£17.99	Oct
Humberside	1-85937-215-5	£14.99	Oct
Manchester (pb)	1-85937-198-1	£9.99	Oct
Middlesex	1-85937-158-2	£14.99	Oct
Norfolk Living Memories	1-85937-217-1	£14.99	Oct
Preston (pb)	1-85937-212-0	£9.99	Oct
South Hams	1-85937-220-1	£14.99	Oct
Suffolk	1-85937-221-x	£9.99	Oct
Swansea (pb)	1-85937-167-1	£9.99	Oct
West Yorkshire (pb)	1-85937-201-5	£9.99	Oct

See Frith books on the internet www.frithbook.co.uk

FRITH PRODUCTS & SERVICES

Francis Frith would doubtless be pleased to know that the pioneering publishing venture he started in 1860 still continues today. A hundred and forty years later, The Francis Frith Collection continues in the same innovative tradition and is now one of the foremost publishers of vintage photographs in the world. Some of the current activities include:

Interior Decoration

Today Frith's photographs can be seen framed and as giant wall murals in thousands of pubs, restaurants, hotels, banks, retail stores and other public buildings throughout the country. In every case they enhance the unique local atmosphere of the places they depict and provide reminders of gentler days in an increasingly busy and frenetic world.

Product Promotions

Frith products are used by many major companies to promote the sales of their own products or to reinforce their own history and heritage. Frith promotions have been used by Hovis bread, Courage beers, Scots Porage Oats, Colman's mustard, Cadbury's foods, Mellow Birds coffee, Dunhill pipe tobacco, Guinness, and Bulmer's Cider.

Genealogy and Family History

As the interest in family history and roots grows world-wide, more and more people are turning to Frith's photographs of Great Britain for images of the towns, villages and streets where their ancestors lived; and, of course, photographs of the churches and chapels where their ancestors were christened, married and buried are an essential part of every genealogy tree and family album.

Frith Products

All Frith photographs are available Framed or just as Mounted Prints and Posters (size 23 x 16 inches). These may be ordered from the address below. From time to time other products - Address Books, Calendars, Table Mats, etc - are available.

The Internet

Already twenty thousand Frith photographs can be viewed and purchased on the internet. By the end of the year 2000 some 60,000 Frith photographs will be available on the internet. The number of sites is constantly expanding, each focussing on different products and services from the Collection.
The main Frith sites are listed below.

www.francisfrith.co.uk
www.frithbook.co.uk

See the complete list of Frith Books at:
www.frithbook.co.uk

This web site is regularly updated with the latest list of publications from the Frith Book Company. If you wish to buy books relating to another part of the country that your local bookshop does not stock, you may purchase on-line.

For further information, trade, or author enquiries please contact us at the address below:
The Francis Frith Collection, Frith's Barn, Teffont, Salisbury, Wiltshire, England SP3 5QP.
Tel: +44 (0)1722 716 376 Fax: +44 (0)1722 716 881 Email: uksales@francisfrith.com

See Frith books on the internet www.frithbook.co.uk

TO RECEIVE YOUR FREE MOUNTED PRINT

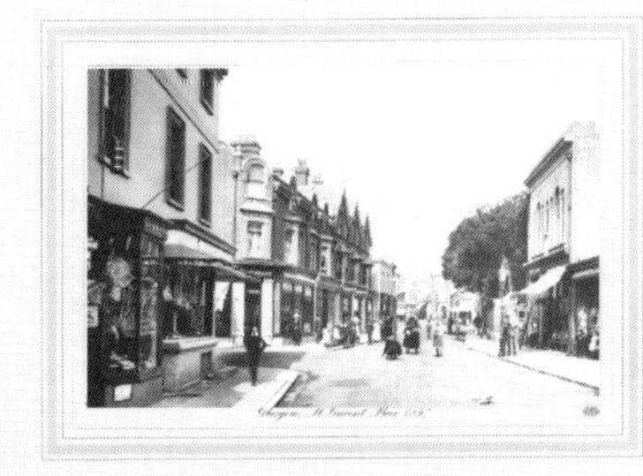

Mounted Print
Overall size 14 x 11 inches

Cut out this Voucher and return it with your remittance for £1.50 to cover postage and handling, to UK addresses. For overseas addresses please include £4.00 post and handling.
Choose any photograph included in this book. Your SEPIA print will be A4 in size, and mounted in a cream mount with burgundy rule lines, overall size 14 x 11 inches.

Order additional Mounted Prints at HALF PRICE (only £7.49 each*)
If there are further pictures you would like to order, possibly as gifts for friends and family, purchase them at half price (no additional postage and handling required).

Have your Mounted Prints framed*
For an additional £14.95 per print you can have your chosen Mounted Print framed in an elegant polished wood and gilt moulding, overall size 16 x 13 inches (no additional postage and handling required).

*** IMPORTANT!**
These special prices are only available if ordered using the original voucher on this page (no copies permitted) and at the same time as your free Mounted Print, for delivery to the same address

Frith Collectors' Guild

From time to time we publish a magazine of news and stories about Frith photographs and further special offers of Frith products. If you would like 12 months FREE membership, please return this form.

Send completed forms to:
The Francis Frith Collection, Frith's Barn, Teffont, Salisbury, Wiltshire SP3 5QP

Voucher for FREE and Reduced Price Frith Prints

Picture no.	Page number	Qty	Mounted @ £7.49	Framed + £14.95	Total Cost
		1	**Free of charge***	£	£
			£7.49	£	£
			£7.49	£	£
			£7.49	£	£
			£7.49	£	£
			£7.49	£	£
Please allow 28 days for delivery			*** Post & handling**		**£1.50**
Book Title			**Total Order Cost**		**£**

Please do not photocopy this voucher. Only the original is valid, so please cut it out and return it to us.

I enclose a cheque / postal order for £ ....
made payable to 'The Francis Frith Collection'
OR please debit my Mastercard / Visa / Switch / Amex card
Number ....
Issue No (Switch only) .... Valid from (Amex/Switch) ....
Expires .... Signature ....
Name Mr/Mrs/Ms ....
Address ....
....
....
....
.... Postcode ....
Daytime Tel No ....

Valid to 31/12/02

The Francis Frith Collectors' Guild

Please enrol me as a member for 12 months free of charge.

Name Mr/Mrs/Ms ....
Address ....
....
....
.... Postcode ....